Elsie de Wolfe

THE HOUSE IN GOOD TASTE

Rizzoli
NEW YORK

What is the goal?

A house that is like the life that goes on with it,
a house that gives us beauty as we understand it—
and beauty of a nobler kind that we may grow to understand,
a house that looks refined.

Published by arrangement with the Elsie de Wolfe Foundation, Inc.

This edition first published in 2004 by
Rizzoli International Publications, Inc.
300 Park Avenue South
New York, NY 10010
www.rizzoliusa.com

De Wolfe, Elsie, The House in Good Taste—Reprint, with a preface and endnotes by Hutton Wilkinson and a foreword by Albert Hadley, Rizzoli International Publications, 2004. First published in 1913 by The Century Co.

Printed and bound in the United States

2005 2006 2007 2008 / 10 9 8 7 6 5 4 3

ISBN: 0-8478-2631-7

Library of Congress Control Number: 2003116890

Rizzoli editor: Eva Prinz
Design by the Simultaneous Workshop

RIZZOLI
NEW YORK

THE HOUSE IN GOOD TASTE

CONTENTS

FOREWORD

ELSIE DE WOLFE'S FIRST BOOK was published in 1913, a few years before I was born, but as a schoolboy I was much more interested in reading—and devouring—*The House in Good Taste* than concentrating on Latin or math. Her chatty and personal guide was provocative, and the clearly worldly and glamorous de Wolfe was onto something as she explored décor and entertainment, orchestrated to the steady cadence, "suitability, suitability, SUITABILITY!"

Since those early days, *The House in Good Taste* has remained on my bookshelf, a constant source of pleasure and inspiration, both of which I've shared with countless students and aspiring decorators.

One of de Wolfe's many quips—which she often had embroidered on small, fat taffeta pillows that punctuated her sofas and chairs—was "Never complain, never explain." No complaints greet *The House in Good Taste*'s reissue, very much in its original form. The re-introduction of de Wolfe and her treatise is undoubtedly of landslide interest to all who missed it the first time around. I know that were she here today, de Wolfe would celebrate, probably with her device of entertainment, an exercise: the famous Elsie de Wolfe headstand.

Albert Hadley
New York, 2004

PREFACE

I WAS IN MY EARLY TEENS perusing a book from my father's architectural library when I first stumbled upon her name. I had no idea who the elegant young woman was in the photograph "Miss Elsie de Wolfe Lounging in her Turkish Corner." Clad in Victorian lace, she sprawled amidst luxurious embroidered cushions arranged on an elaborately patterned Persian rug under a fringed and tasseled Oriental awning. The photo was taken while she was known only as "the best dressed star on Broadway," before she invented the profession known as "the interior designer." Its garish décor represented everything she loathed and was soon to sweep away.

Born in New York City in 1865, Elsie de Wolfe would refer to herself as "an ugly child born in an ugly age." Her parents moved the outspoken child from one unattractive house to another; only European jaunts exposed de Wolfe to the fineries of the home, such as that of her uncle Archibald Hamilton Charteris, chaplain to Queen Victoria at Scotland's Balmoral Castle. A twenty-year-old de Wolfe was later presented to Queen Victoria at Buckingham Palace as a young debutante, imparting her with a special luster upon her return to New York.

De Wolfe the young socialite partook in amateur theatricals and charity work until her father's death in 1890, at which time she became her family's breadwinner, turning her talents to the professional stage. She gained a contract with the great theatrical impresario Charles Frohman, who recognized that although de Wolfe was neither a great beauty nor a talented actress, she definitely knew how to wear a dress.

The "best dressed star on Broadway" soon set up bachelorette residence at the historic Washington Irving House with her friend, Miss Elizabeth Marbury, a prominent theatrical agent at the turn of the century, an influential power broker within the Democratic party, and, along with de Wolfe, a supporter of women's rights. The combination of de Wolfe's style and Marbury's connections transformed the Irving House into an American version of a European salon, their soirees attracting a panoply of international visitors such as Sarah Bernhardt, Oscar Wilde, Victorien Sardou, J.P. Morgan, Ethel Barrymore, and Mrs. William Waldorf Astor. During this time, de Wolfe became a student of the decorative arts, renovating the interiors of the Irving House to better suit her and Bessy's new European aesthetic. Her creative and individual interiors at the Irving House were a social success, and soon she invented the business of charging her friends for her decorative savoir faire, a heretofore unheard-of notion.

De Wolfe's idea to decorate her friends' houses was an instant success. Alone in her field for many years, she corralled her well-heeled friends on both coasts, sweeping out their dark and fussy Victorian furnishings and replacing them with arrangements, materials, and styles that have become the foundations of modern interiors. A woman who knew her worth and was not afraid to charge for it, de Wolfe quickly amassed a fortune that she used to cultivate a lifestyle that her clients wanted to emulate. Realizing the value of publicity and embracing it wholeheartedly, de Wolfe saw everyone and anyone who could afford her acquired tastes. After decorating New York's Colony Club and the Henry Clay Frick residence (now the Frick Collection), de Wolfe cemented her reputation as an arbiter of taste through a series of articles for the magazine *The Delineator*. De Wolfe later compiled these articles into *The House in Good Taste*, first published in 1913.

In 1969, many years after discovering de Wolfe in the aforementioned photograph, I decided to pursue a career in interior design. And as a seventeen-year-old boy in Los Angeles, I made a wish list of my favorite tastemakers in hopes of one day meeting them: Tony Duquette, Cecil Beaton, Oliver Messel, the Baron de Rede, and Carlos de Beistegui. All of these men were de Wolfe's close personal friends, Duquette her last great protégé. She discovered him after moving to Beverly Hills when her Versaille house, the Villa Trianon, had been taken over by Nazis during the Second World War. She never tired of proclaiming Duquette a genius, and when the war was over in 1947 she took him to Europe with her and her husband Sir Charles Mendl, where they introduced Duquette to their continental friends. (Duquette and his wife Elizabeth were with de Wolfe when she died in Paris in 1950.)

As an eighteen-year-old aspiring designer I was fortunate to meet and work for Tony Duquette, first as an apprentice and later as his business partner. Over the next thirty years I was enthralled to hear amusing de Wolfe anecdotes—from Duquette (who de Wolfe affectionately called "the kid" and "the only one" because she had so many Tonys in her life), his wife Elizabeth, and others of that generation who had also known de Wolfe. Through Duquette, I was fortunate enough to meet the other icons on my wish list (save de Beistegui), and visit the Villa Trianon, which, thirty years after her death, was exactly as de Wolfe had lived in it, a testament to her timeless taste.

In her will de Wolfe left her fortune to the Elsie de Wolfe Foundation, a non-profit private foundation dedicated to advancing the decorative arts in America. Her trusted secretary Hilda West was the foundation's first president, followed by Duquette, and upon his 1999 passing, the Board of Directors asked me to take the position.

In keeping with our founders' wishes, it has been the foundation's pleasure to sponsor scholarships, exhibitions, and publications on the decorative arts, as well as permanent installations in museums and public spaces across America. It is our hope that this reprinted edition of *The House in Good Taste* will continue to inspire individuality and creativity, which Elsie de Wolfe here writes about, in students, homemakers, and professional designers, not only in America but around the world.

Hutton Wilkinson, President
The Elsie de Wolfe Foundation

THE HOUSE
IN
GOOD TASTE

I.
THE DEVELOPMENT OF THE MODERN HOUSE

I KNOW OF NOTHING MORE SIGNIFICANT than the awakening of men and women throughout our country to the desire to improve their houses. Call it what you will—awakening, development, American Renaissance—it is a most startling and promising condition of affairs.

It is no longer possible, even to people of only faintly aesthetic tastes, to buy chairs merely to sit upon or a clock merely that it should tell the time. Homemakers are determined to have their houses, outside and in, correct according to the best standards. What do we mean by the best standards? Certainly not those of the useless, overcharged house of the average American millionaire, who builds and furnishes his home with a hopeless disregard for tradition. We must accept the standards that the artists and the architects accept, the standards that have come to us from those exceedingly rational people, our ancestors.

Our ancestors built for stability and use, and so their simple houses were excellent examples of architecture. Their spacious, uncluttered interiors were usually beautiful. Houses and furniture fulfilled their uses, and if an object fulfills its mission, the chances are that it is beautiful.

It is all very well to plan our ideal house or apartment, our individual castle in Spain, but it isn't necessary to live among intolerable furnishings just because we cannot realize our castle. There never was a house so bad that it couldn't be made over into something worthwhile.

We shall all be very much happier when we learn to transform the things we have into a semblance of our ideal. How, then, may we go about accomplishing our ideal?

By letting it go!

By forgetting this vaguely pleasing dream, this evidence of our smug vanity, and making ourselves ready for a new ideal.

By considering the body of material from which it is good sense to choose when we have a house to decorate.

By studying the development of the modern house, its romantic tradition and architectural history.

By taking upon ourselves the duty of self-taught lessons of sincerity and common sense, and suitability.

By learning what is meant by color and form and line, harmony and contract and proportion.

When we are on familiar terms with our tools, and feel our vague ideas clearing into definite inspiration, then we are ready to talk about our ideals. We are fit to approach the full art of homemaking.

We take it for granted that everyone is interested in houses—that she either has a house in course of construction, or dreams of having one, or has had a house long enough wrong to wish it right. And we take it for granted that the American home was always the woman's home: a man may build and decorate a beautiful house, but it remains for a woman to make a home of it for him. It was the personality of the mistress that the home expressed. Men are forever guests in our homes, no matter how much happiness they may find there.[1]

You will express yourself in your home, whether you want to or not, so you must make up your mind to a long preparatory discipline. You may have only one house to furnish in your lifetime, possibly, so be careful and go warily. Therefore, you must select for your architect a person who isn't too determined to their way. It is a fearful mistake to leave the entire planning of your home to a person whose social experience may be limited, for instance, for they can impose on you their conception of your tastes with a damning permanency and emphasis. I once heard a certain Boston architect say that he taught his clients to be ladies and gentlemen. He couldn't, you know. All he could do was to set the front door so that it would reprove them if they weren't!

Who does not know, for instance, those mistaken people whose houses represent their own or their architects' hasty visits to the fine old châteaux of the Loire, or the palaces of Versailles, or the fine old houses of England, or the gracious villas of Italy? We must avoid such aspiring architects, and visualize our homes not as so many specially designated rooms and convenient closets, but as individual expressions of ourselves, of the future we plan, of our dreams for our children. The ideal house is the house that has been long planned for, long awaited.

Fortunately for us, our best architects are so very good that we are better than safe if we take our problems to them. These people associate with themselves the hundred architects who are eager to prove themselves on small houses. The idea that it is economical to be your own architect and trust your house to a building contractor is a mistaken, and most expensive one. The surer you are of your architect's common sense and professional ability, the surer you may be that your house will be economically efficient. They will not only plan a house that will meet the needs of your family, but they will also give your inspiration for its interior. They will concern themselves with the moldings, the light-openings, the door handles, and hinges, the unconsidered things that make or mar your house. Select for your architect a person you'd like for a friend. Perhaps he or she will be, before the house comes true. If you are both sincere, if you both purpose to have the best thing you can afford, the house will express genius and character of your architect and the personality and character of yourself, as a great painting suggests both painter and sitter. The hard won triumph of a well-built house means many compromises, but the ultimate satisfaction is worth everything.[2]

I do not purpose, in this book, to go into historic traditions of architecture and decoration—there are so many excellent books it were absurd to review them—but I do wish to trace briefly the development of the modern house, the woman's house, to show you that all that is intimate and charming in the home as we know it, has come through the unmeasured influence of women. Man conceived the great house with its parade rooms, its *grands appartements* but woman found eternal paradise tiresome, and planned for herself little retreats, rooms small enough for comfort and intimacy. In short, man made the house: woman went him one better and made it a home.[3]

The virtues of simplicity and reticence in form first came into being, as nearly as we can tell, in the *Grotta*, the little studio-like apartment of Isabella d'Este, the Marchioness of Mantua, away back in 1496. The Marchioness made of this little studio her personal retreat. Here she brought many of the treasures of the Italian Renaissance. Really, simplicity and reticence were that last things she considered, but the point is that they were considered at all in such a restless, passionate age. Later, in 1522, she established the *Paradiso*, a suite of apartments, which she occupied after her husband's death. So you see the idea of a woman planning her own apartment is pretty old after all.[4]

The next woman who took a stand that revealed genuine social consciousness was that half-French, half-Italian woman, Catherine de Vivonne, Marquise de Rambouillet. She seceded from court because the court was swaggering and hurly-burly, with florid Marie-de-Medicis at its head. And with this recession, she began to express in her conduct, her feeling, her conversation, and finally, in her house, her awakened consciousness of beauty and reserve, of simplicity and suitability.

This was the early seventeenth century, mind you, when the main salons of the French houses were filled with such institutions as rows of red chairs and boxed state beds. She undertook, first of all, to have a light and gracefully curving stairway leading to her salon instead of supplanting it. She grouped her rooms with a lovely diversity of size and purpose, whereas before they had been vast, stately halls with cubbies hardby for sleeping. She gave the bedroom its alcove, boudoir, antechamber, and even its bath, and then as decorator she supplanted the old feudal yellow and red with her famous silver-blue. She covered blue chairs with silver bullion. She fashioned long, tenderly colored curtains of novel shades. Reticence was always in evidence, but it was the reticence of elegance. It was through Madame de Rambouillet that the armchair received its final distribution of yielding parts, and began to express the comfort of soft padded backward slope, of width and warmth and color.

It was all very heavy, very grave, very angular, this Hôtel Rambouillet, but it was devised for and consecrated to conversation, considered a new form of privilege! The *précieuses* in their later jargon called chairs "the indispensables of conversation."

I have been at some length to give a picture of Madame de Rambouillet's hôtel because it really is the earliest modern house. There, where the society that frequented it was analyzing its soul in dialogue and long platonic discussion that would seem stark enough to us, the word which it invented for itself was *urbanité*—the coinage of one of its own foremost figures.

It is unprofitable to follow on into the grandeurs of Louis XIV, if one hopes to find an advance there in truth-telling architecture. At the end of that splendid official success the squalor of Versailles was unspeakable, its stenches unbearable. In spite of its size, the Palace was known as the most comfortless house in Europe. After the death of its owner, society, in a fit of madness, plunged into the *rocaille*. When the restlessness of Louis XV could no longer find moorings in this brilliancy, there came into being little houses called folies, garden hemitages for the privileged. Here we find Madame de Pompadour in calicoes, in a wild garden, barefoot, playing as a milkmaid, or seated in a little gray-white interior with painted wooden furniture, having her supper on an earthen-ware service that has replaced old silver and gold. Amorous alcoves lost their painted Loves and took on gray and white decorations. The casinos of little *comédiennes* did not glitter any more. English sentiment began to bedim Gallic eyes, and so what we know as the Louis XVI style was born.

And so, at that moment, the idea of the modern house came into its own. And it could advance—as an idea—hardly any further. For with all the intrepidity and passion of the later eighteenth century in its search for beauty, for all the magic-making of convenience and ingenuity of the nineteenth dentury, the fundamentals have changed but little. And now we of the twentieth century can only add material comforts as an expression of our personality. We raise the house beyond the reach of squalor, we give it measured heat, we give it water in abundance and perfect sanitation and light everywhere, we give it ventilation, and finally we give it the human quality that is so modern. There are no dungeons in the good modern house, no disgraceful lairs for housekeepers, no horrors of humidity.

And so we have achieved a house, luminous with kind purpose throughout. It is finished—that is our difficulty! We inherit it, all rounded in its perfection, consummate in its charms, but it is finished, and what can we do about a thing that is finished? Doesn't it seem that we are back in the old position of Isabella d'Este—eager, predatory, and "thingy"? And isn't it time for us to pull up short least we sidestep the goal? We are so sure of a thousand appetites we are in danger of passing by the amiable commonplaces. We find ourselves dismayed in old houses that look too simple. We must stop and ask ourselves questions, and, if necessary, plan for ourselves little retreats until we can find ourselves again.

What is the goal? A house that is like the life that goes on with it, a house that gives us beauty as we understand it—and beauty of a nobler kind that we may grow to understand, a house that looks refined.

Suppose you have obtained this sort of wisdom—a sane viewpoint. I think it will give you as great a satisfaction to re-arrange your house with what you have. The results may not be so charming, but you can learn by them. You can take your indiscriminate inheritance of Victorian rosewood of Eastlake walnut and cocobolo, your pickle-and-plum colored Morris furniture, and make a civilized interior by placing it right. And putting detail at the right points. Your sense of the pleasure and meaning of human intercourse will be clear in your disposition of your best things, in your elimination of your worst ones.[5]

When you have emptied the table of rubbish so that you can put things down on them at need, place them in light where you can write on them in repose, or isolate real works of art in the middle of them; when you have set your upholstered sofas where you want them for talk, or warmth and reading; when you can see the fire from the bed in your sleeping room, and dress near your bath; this is a sense of your rights as acknowledged by your arrangements, with this in mind your rooms will always have meaning in the end. If you like only the things in a chair that have meaning, and grow to hate the rest you will, without any other instruction, prefer—the next time you are buying—a good Louis XVI *fauteuil* guilty of the errors of meaningless magnificence.[6]

To most of us in America who must perforce lead workaday lives, the absence of beauty is a very distinct lack. I think, indeed, that the present awakening has come to stay, and that before very long, we shall have simple houses with fireplaces that draw, electric lights in the proper places, comfortable and sensible furniture, and not a gilt-legged spindle-shanked table or chair anywhere. This may be a decorator's optimistic dream, but let us all hope that it may come true.

II.
SUITABILITY, SIMPLICITY AND PROPORTION

When I am asked to decorate a new house, my first thought is suitability. My next thought is proportion. Always I keep in mind the importance of simplicity. First, I study the people who are to live in this house, and their needs, as thoroughly as I studied my parts in the days when I was an actress. For the time being I really am the *chatelaine* of the house. When I have thoroughly familiarized myself with the "part," I let that go for the time, and consider the proportion of the house and its rooms. It is much more important that the wall openings, windows, doors, and fireplaces should be in the right place and should balance one another than that there should be expensive and extravagant hangings and carpets.

My first thought in laying out a room is the placing of the electric light openings. How rarely does one find the lights in the right place in our over-magnificent hotels and residences! One arrives from a journey tired out and travel-stained, only to find oneself facing a mirror as far removed from the daylight as possible, with the artificial lights directly behind one, or high in the ceiling in the center of the room. In my houses I always see that each room shall have its lights placed for the comfort of its occupants. There must be lights in sheltered corners of the fireplace, by the writing desk, on each side of the dressing table, and so on.[1]

Then I consider the heating of the room. We Americans are slaves to steam heat. We ruin our furniture, our complexions, and our dispositions by this enervating atmosphere of too much heat. In my own houses

I have a fireplace in each room, and I burn wood in it. There is a heating system in the basement of my house, but it is under perfect control. I prefer the normal heat of sunshine and open fires. But, granted that open fires are impossible in all your rooms, do arrange in the beginning that the small rooms of your house may not be overheated. It is a distinct irritation to a person who loves clean air to go into a room where a flood of steam heat pours out of every corner. There is usually no way to control it unless you turn it off altogether. I once had the temerity to do this in a certain hotel room where there was a cold and cheerless empty fireplace. I summoned a reluctant chambermaid, only to be told that the chimney had never had a fire in it and the proprietor would rather not take such a risk! Perhaps the guests in your house would not be so troublesome, but don't tempt them! If you have a fireplace, see that it is in working order.[2]

We are sure to judge a person in whose house we find ourselves for the first time, by their surroundings. We judge their temperament, their habits, their inclinations, by the interior of their home. We may talk of the weather, but we are looking at the furniture. We attribute vulgar qualities to those who are content to live in ugly surroundings. We endow with refinement and charm the person who welcomes us in a delightful room, where the colors blend and the proportions are as perfect as in a picture. After all, what surer guarantee can there be of a person's character, natural and cultivated, inherent and inherited, than taste? It is a compass that never errs. When people have taste they may have faults, follies, fads, they may err, they may be as human and honest as they please, but they will never cause a scandal!

How can we develop taste? Some of us, alas, can never develop it, because we can never let go of shams. We must learn to recognize suitability, simplicity and proportion, and apply our knowledge to our needs. I grant you we may never fully appreciate the full balance of proportion, but we can exert our common sense and decide whether a thing is suitable; we can consult our conscience as to whether an object is simple, and we can train our eyes to recognize good and bad proportion. A technical knowledge of architecture is not necessary to know that a huge stuffed leather chair in a tiny gold and cream room is unsuitable, is hideously complicated, and is as much out of proportion as the proverbial bull in the china shop.

A person's environment will speak for their life, whether they like it or not. How can we believe that a person of sincerity of purpose will hang fake "works of art" on their walls or satisfy themselves with imitation velvets or silks? How can we attribute taste to a person who permits paper floors and iron ceilings in their house?[3] We are too afraid of the restful commonplaces, and yet if we live simple lives, why shouldn't we be glad our houses are comfortably commonplace? How much better to have plain furniture that is comfortable, simple chintzes printed from old blocks, a few good prints, than all the sham things in the world? A house is a dead giveaway, anyhow, so you should arrange it so that the person who sees your personality in it will be reassured, not disconcerted.

Too often in America, the most comfortable room in the house is given up to a sort of bastard collection of gilt chairs and tables, over-elaborate draperies shutting out both light and air, and huge and frightful paintings. This style of room, with its museum-like furnishings, has been dubbed "Marie Antoinette"—why, no one but the American decorator can say. Heaven knows poor Marie Antoinette had enough follies to atone for, but certainly she has never been treated more shabbily than when they dub these mausoleums "Marie Antoinette rooms."[4] I remember taking a clever Englishwoman of much taste to see a woman who was very proud of her new house. We had seen most of the house when the hostess, who had evidently reserved what she considered the best for the last, threw open the doors of a large and gorgeous apartment and said, "This is my Louis XVI ballroom." My friend, who had been very patient up to that moment, said very quietly, "What makes you think so?"

Louis XVI thought a salon well-furnished with a few fine chairs and a table. He wished to be of supreme importance. In the immense salons of the Italian palaces there were a few benches and chairs. People then wished spaces about them.

Nowadays, people are swamped by their furniture. Too many centuries, too many races, crowd one another in a small room. The owner seems insignificant among these collections of historical furniture. Whether they collect all sorts of things of all periods in one heterogeneous mass, or whether they fill their house with the furniture of some one epoch, *they* are not at home in their surroundings.

The furniture of every epoch records its history. Our ancestors of the fourteenth and fifteenth centuries inherited the troublesome times of their families in their heavy oaken chests. They owned more chests than anything else, because a chest could be carried away on the back of a sturdy pack mule, when the necessity arose for flight.

People never had time to sit down in the sixteenth century. Their feverish unrest is recorded in their stiff-backed chairs. It was not until the seventeenth century that they had time to sit down and talk. We need no book of history to teach us this – we have only to observe the ample proportions of the armchairs of the period.

Our ancestors of the seventeenth and eighteenth centuries worked with a faith in the permanence of what they created. We have lost this happy confidence. We are occupied exclusively with preserving and reproducing. We have not succeeded in creating a style adapted to our modern life. It is just as well! Our life, with its haste, its nervousness and its preoccupations does not inspire the furniture makers. We cannot do better than to accept the standards of other times, and adapt them to our uses.[5]

Why should we Americans run after styles and periods of which we know nothing? Why should we not be content with the fundamental things? The formal French room is very delightful in the proper place, but when it is unsuited to the people who must live in it, it is just as bad as a sham room. The woman who wears paste jewels is not so conspicuously wrong as the woman who plasters herself with too many real jewels at the wrong time!

This is what I am always fighting in people's houses: the unsuitability of things. The foolish person goes about from shop to shop and buys as their fancy directs. They see something "pretty" and buy it, though it has no reference either in form or color to the scheme of their house. Haven't you been in rooms where there was a jumble of mission furniture, satinwood, fine old mahogany and gilt-legged chairs? And it is the same with color. Someone says "Oh, I love blue, let's have blue!" regardless of the exposure of their room and the furnishings they have already collected. And then, when they have treated each one of their rooms in a different color, and with a different floor covering, they wonder why they always fret going from one room to another.

Don't go about the furnishing of your house with the idea that you must select the furniture of some one period and stick to that. It isn't at all necessary. There are old English chairs and tables of the sixteenth and seventeenth centuries that fit into our quiet, spacious twentieth-century country homes. Lines and fabrics and woods are the things to be compared.

There are so many beautiful things that have come to us from other times that it should be easy to make our homes beautiful, but I have seen what I can best describe as apoplectic chairs whose legs were fashioned like aquatic plants; tables upheld by tortured naked women; lighting fixtures in the form of tassels, and such horrors, in many houses of today under the guise of being "authentic period furniture." Only a *connoisseur* can ever hope to know about the furniture of every period, but all of us can easily learn the earmarks of the furniture that is suited to our homes. I shan't talk about earmarks here, however, because dozens of collectors have compiled excellent books that tell you all about curves and lines and woodgrain and wormholes. My business is to persuade you to use your graceful French sofas and your simple rush-bottom New England chairs in different rooms—in other words, to preach to you the beauty of suitability.

SUITABILITY! *Suitability!* SUITABILITY![6]

It is such a relief to return to the tranquil, simple forms of furniture, and to decorate our rooms by a process of elimination. How many rooms have I not cleared of junk—this heterogeneous mass of ornamental "period" furniture and bric-a-brac bought to make a room "look cozy." Once cleared of these, the simplicity and dignity of the room comes back, the architectural spaces are freed and now stand in their proper relation to the furniture. In other words, the architecture of the room becomes its decoration.

III.
THE OLD WASHINGTON IRVING HOUSE

I HAVE ALWAYS LIVED in enchanting houses. Probably when another woman would be dreaming of love affairs, I dream of the delightful houses I have lived in. And just as the woman who dreams of many lovers finds one dream a little dearer than all the rest, so one of my houses has been dearer to me than all the others.

This favorite love of mine is the old Washington Irving House in New York, the quaint mansion that gave historic Irving Place its name. For twenty years my friend, Elizabeth Marbury, and I made this old house our home. Two years ago we reluctantly gave up the old house and moved into a more modern one—also transformed from old into new—on East Fifty-fifth Street. We have also a delightful old house in France, the Villa Trianon, at Versailles, where we spend our summers. So you see we have had the rare experience of transforming three mistreated old houses into very delightful homes.

When we found this old house, so many years ago, we were very young, and it is amusing now to think of its evolution. We had so many dreams, so many theories, and we tried them all out on the old house. And like a patient, well-bred maiden aunt, the old house always accepted our changes most placidly. There never was such a house!

You could do anything to it, because, fundamentally, it was good. Its wall spaces were inviting, its windows were made for framing pleasant things. When we moved there we had a broad sweep of view; I can remember seeing the river from our dining room. Now the city has grown up around the old house and jostled it rudely, and shut out much of its sunshine.

There is a joy in the opportunity of creating a beautiful interior for a new and up-to-date house, but best of all is the joy of furnishing an old house like this one. It is like reviving an old garden. It may not be just your idea of a garden to begin with, but as you study it and deck its barren spaces with masses of color, and fit a sundial into the spot that so needs it, and give the sunshine a fountain to play with, you love the old garden just a little more every time you touch it, until it becomes to you the most beautiful garden in the world.

Gardens and houses are such whimsical things! This old house of ours had been so long mistreated that it was fairly petulant and querulous when I began studying it. It asked questions on every turn, and seemed surprised when they were answered. The house was delightfully rambling, with a tiny entrance hall, and narrow stairs, and sudden up-and-down steps from one room to another like the old, old house one associates with faraway places and old times.[1]

The little entrance hall was worse than a question, it was a problem, but I finally solved it. The floor was paved with little hexagon-shaped tiles of a wonderful old red. A door made of little square panes of mirrors was placed where it would deceive the old hall into thinking itself a spacious thing. The walls were covered with a green-and-white-stripe wallpaper that looked as old as Rip Van Winkle. This is the same ribbon-grass paper that I afterward used in the Colony Club hallway. The woodwork was painted a soft gray-green. Finally, I had my collection of faded French costume prints set flat against the top of the wall as a frieze. The hall was so very narrow that as you went up stairs you could actually examine the old prints in detail. Another little thing: I covered the handrail of the stairs with a soft gray-green velvet of the same tone as the woodwork, and the effect was so very good and the touch of it so very nice that many of my friends straightaway adopted the idea.[2]

But I am placing the cart before the horse! I should talk of the shell of the house before the contents, shouldn't I? It is hard to talk of this particular house as a thing apart from its furnishings, however, for every bit of paneling, every lighting-fixture, the placing of each mirror, was worked out so that the shell of the house and its furnishings might be in perfect harmony.[3]

The drawing room and dining room occupied the first floor of the house. The drawing room was a long, narrow room with cream woodwork and walls. The walls were broken into panels by the use of a narrow molding. In the large panel above the mantel, I had inset a painting by Nattier.[4]

The color scheme of rose and cream and dull yellow was worked out from the rose and yellow Persian rug. Most of the furniture we found in France, but it fitted perfectly into this aristocratic and dignified room. Miss Marbury and I have a perfect right to French things in our drawing room, you see, for we are French residents for half the year. And, besides, this gracious old house welcomed a fine old Louis XIV sofa as serenely as you please. I have no idea of swallowing my words about unsuitability![5]

Light, air and comfort—these three things I must always have in a room, whether it be drawing room or housekeeper's room. This room had all three. The chairs were all comfortable, the lights well-placed, and there was plenty of sunshine and air. The color of the room was so subdued that it was restful to the eye—one color faded into another so subtly that one did not realize there was a definite color scheme. The hangings of the room were of a deep rose color. I used the same colors in the coverings of the chairs and sofas. The house was curtained throughout with fine white muslin curtains. No matter what the inner curtains of a room may be, I use this simple stuff against the window itself. There isn't any nicer material. To me there is something unsuitable in an array of lace against a window, like underclothes hung up to dry.

The most delightful part of the drawing room was the little conservatory, which was a plain, lamentable bay window once upon a time. I determined to make a little flower-box of it, and had the floor of it paved with large tiles, and between the hardwood floor of the drawing room and the marble of the window space was a narrow curb of marble, which made it possible to have a jolly little fountain in the window. The fountain splashed away to its heart's content, for there was a drain pipe under the curb. At the top of the windows there were shallow white boxes filled with trailing ivy that hung down and screened the glass, making the window as delightful to the passerby without as to us within. There were several pots of rose-colored flowers standing in a prim row on the marble curb.

You see how much simpler it is to make the best of an old bay window than to build on a new conservatory. There are thousands of houses with windows like this one of ours, an unfortunate space of which no use is made. Sometimes there is a gilt table bearing a lofty jar, sometimes a timid effort at comfort—a sofa—but usually the bay window is sacred to its own devices, whatever they may be! Why not spend a few dollars and make it the most interesting part of the room by giving it a lot of vines and flowers and a small fountain? It isn't at all an expensive thing to do.

From the drawing room you entered the dining room. This was a long room with beautifully spaced walls, a high ceiling, and quaint cupboards. The arrangement of the mirrors around the cupboards and doors was unusual and most decorative. This room was so beautiful in itself that I used very little color—but such color! We never tired of the gray and white and ivory color scheme, the quiet atmosphere that made glorious the old Chinese carpet, with its rose-colored ground and blue-and-gold medallions and border. The large India-ink sketches set in the walls are originals by Mennoyer, the delightful eighteenth-century artist who did the overdoors of the Petit Trianon.

The mirror-framed lighting fixtures I brought over from France. The dining table, too, was French, of a creamy ivory-painted wood. The chairs had insets of cane of a deeper tone. The recessed window seat was covered with soft velvet of deep yellow, and there were as many little footstools beside the window seat as there were chairs in the room. Doesn't everyone long for a footstool at the table?

I believe that everything in one's house should be comfortable, but one's bedroom must be more than comfortable: it must be intimate, personal, one's secret garden, so to speak. It may be as simple as a convent cell and still have this quality of the personality of its occupant.

There are two things that are as important to me as the bed in the bedrooms that I furnish, and they are the little tables at the head of the bed, and the lounging chairs. The little table must hold a good reading light, well-shaded, for who doesn't like to read in bed? There must also be a clock, and there really should be a telephone.[6] And the *chaise-longue*, or couch, as the case may be, should be both comfortable and beautiful. Who hasn't longed for a comfortable place to snatch forty winks at midday?[7]

My own bedroom in this house was very pleasant to me. The house was very small, you see, and my bedroom had to be my writing and reading rooms too, so that accounts for the bookshelves that fill the wall space above and around the mantel and the large writing table. The room was built around a wonderful old French bed which came from Brittany. This old bed is of carved mahogany, with mirrored panels on the side against the wall, and with tall columns at the ends. It is always hung with embroidered silk in the rose color that I adore and has any number of pillows, big and little. The *chaise-longue* was covered with this same silk, as were the various chair cushions. The other furnishings were in keeping. It was a delightfully comfortable room, and it grew a little at a time. I needed bookshelves, and I built them. A drop-light was necessary, and I found the old brass lantern which hung from the ceiling. And so it was furnished, bit by bit, need by need.

Miss Marbury's bedroom in this house was entirely different in type, but exactly the same in comfort. The furniture was of white enamel, the walls ivory white, and the rug a soft dull blue. The chintz used was the familiar Bird of Paradise, gorgeous in design, but so subdued in tone that one never tires of it. The bed had a flat, perfectly fitted cover of the chintz, which is tucked under the mattress. The box spring was also covered with the chintz, and the effect was always tidy and satisfactory. This is the neatest disposal of the bedclothes I have seen. I always advise this arrangement.[7]

Besides the bed there was the necessary little table, holding a reading light and so forth, and at the head of the bed a most adorable screen of white enamel, paneled with chintz below and glass above. There was a soft couch of generous width in this room, with covers and cushions of chintz.

Over near the windows was the dressing table with the lighting fixtures properly placed. This table, hung with chintz, had a sheet of plate glass exactly fitting its top. The writing table, near the window, is also part of my creed of comfort. There should be a writing table in every bedroom. My friends laugh at the little fat pincushions on my writing tables, but when they are covered with a bit of the chintz or tapestry or brocade of the room they are very pretty, and I am sure pins are as necessary on the writing table as on the dressing table.

Another thing I like on every writing table is a clear glass bowl of dried rose petals, which gives the room the faintest spicy fragrance. There is also a little bowl of just the proper color to hold pens and clips and odds and ends. I get as much pleasure from planning these small details as from the planning of the larger furniture in every room.

The house was very simple, you see, and very small, so when the time came to leave it we had grown to love every inch of it. You can love a small house so completely! But we couldn't forgive the skyscrapers encroaching on our supply of sunshine, and we really needed more room, and so we said goodbye to our beloved old house and moved into a new one. Now we find ourselves in danger of loving the new one as much as the old. But that is another story.

IV.
THE LITTLE HOUSE OF MANY MIRRORS

One walks the streets of New York and receives the fantastic impression that some giant architect has made for the city thousands of houses in replica. These dismal brownstone buildings are so alike within, that one wonders how their owners know their homes from one another. I have had the pleasure of making over many of these gloomy barracks into homes for other people, and when we left the old Irving Place House we took one of these dreary houses for ourselves, and made it over into a semblance of what a city house should be.

You know the kind of house—there are tens of thousands of them—a four-story and basement house of pinkish brownstone, with a long flight of ugly stairs from the street to the first floor. The common belief that all city houses of this type must be dark and dreary just because they always have been dark and dreary is an unnecessary superstition.

My object in taking this house was twofold: I wanted to prove to my friends that it was possible to take one of the darkest and grimiest of city houses and make it an abode of sunshine and light, and I wanted to furnish the whole house exactly as I pleased—for once!

The remaking of the house was very interesting. I tore away the ugly stone steps and centered the entrance door in a little stone-paved fore-court on the level of the old area-way. The fore-court is just a step below street level, giving you a pleasant feeling of invitation. Everyone hates to climb into a house, but there is a subtle allure in a garden or a courtyard or a room into which you must step down. The fore-court is enclosed with a high iron railing banked with formal box-trees. Above the huge green entrance door there is a graceful iron balcony, filled with green things, that pulls the great door and the central window of the floor above into an impressive composition. The façade of the house, instead of being a commonplace rectangle of stone broken by windows, has this long connected break of the door and balcony and window. By such simple devices are happy results accomplished![1]

The door itself is noteworthy, with its great bronze knob set squarely in the center. On each side of it there are the low windows of the entrance hall, with window boxes of evergreens. Compare this orderly arrangement of windows and entrance door with the badly balanced houses of the old type, and you will realize anew the value of balance and proportion.

From the fore-court you enter the hall. Once within the hall, the house widens magically. Surely this cool black and white apartment cannot be a part of restless New York! Have you ever come suddenly upon an old Southern house, and thrilled at the classic purity of white columns in a black-green forest? This entrance hall gives you the same thrill; the elements of formality, of tranquility, of coolness, are so evident. The walls and ceiling are a deep, flat cream, and the floor is laid in large black and white marble tiles. Exactly opposite as you enter, there is a wall fountain with a background of mirrors. The water spills over from the fountain into ferns and flowers banked within a marble curb. The two wall spaces on your right and left are broken by graceful niches which hold old statues. An oval Chinese rug and the white and orange flowers of the fountain furnish the necessary color. The windows flanking the entrance doorway are hung with flat curtains of coarse white linen, with inserts of old filet lace, and there are side curtains of dead black silk with borders of silver and gold threads.

In any house that I have anything to do with, there is some sort of desk or table for writing in the hall. How often I have been in other people's houses when it was necessary to send a message, or to record an address, when the whole household began scurrying around trying to find a pencil and paper! This, to my mind, is an outward and visible sign of an inward—and fundamental!—lack of order.

In this hall there is a charming desk particularly adapted to its place. It is a standing desk which can be lowered or heightened at will, so that one who wishes to scribble a line or so may use it without sitting down. This desk is called a *bureau d'architect.* I found it in Biarritz. It would be quite easy to have one made by a good cabinet-maker, for the lines and method of construction are simple. My hall desk is so placed that it is lighted by the window by day and the wall lights by night, but it might be lighted by two tall candlesticks if a wall light were not available. There is a shallow drawer which contains surplus writing materials, but the only things permitted on the writing surface of the desk are the tray for cards, the pad and pencils. The only other furniture in the hall is an old porter's chair near the door, a chair that suggests the sedan of old France, but serves its purpose admirably.

A glass door leads to the inner hall and the stairway, which I consider the best thing in the house. Instead of the usual steep and gloomy stairs with which we are all familiar, here is a graceful spiral stairway which runs from this floor to the roof. The stair hall has two walls made up of mirrors in the French fashion, that is, cut in squares and held in place by small rosettes of gilt, and these mirrored walls seemingly double the spaciousness of what would be, under ordinary conditions, a gloomy inside hallway.[2]

The house is narrow in the extreme, and the secret of its successful renaissance is plenty of windows and mirrors—mirrors—mirrors! It has been called the "Little House of Many Mirrors," for so much of its spaciousness and charm is the effect of skillfully managed reflections. The stair landings are most ingeniously planned. There are landings that lead directly from the stairs into the rooms of each floor, and back of one of the mirrored stair walls there is a little balcony connecting the rooms on that floor, a private passageway.

The drawing room and dining room occupy the first floor. The drawing room is a pleasant, friendly place, full of quiet color. The walls are a deep cream color and the floor is covered with a beautiful Savonnerie rug. There are many beautiful old chairs covered with Aubusson tapestry, and other chairs and sofas covered with rose-colored brocade. The drawing room is seemingly a huge place, this effect being given by the careful placing of mirrors and lights, and the skillful arrangement of the furniture. I believe in plenty of optimism and white paint, comfortable chairs with lights beside them, open fires on the hearth and flowers wherever they "belong," mirrors and sunshine in all rooms.

But I think we can carry the white paint idea too far: I have grown a little tired of over-careful decorations, of plain white walls, and white woodwork, of carefully matched furniture and over-cautious color schemes. Somehow the feeling of hominess is lost when the decorator is too careful. In this drawing room there is furniture of many woods, there are stuffs of many weaves, there are candles and chandeliers and reading lamps, but there is harmony of purpose and therefore harmony of effect. The room was made for conversation, for hospitality.

A narrow landing connects the dining room and the drawing room. The color of the dining room has grown of itself, from the superb Chinese rug on the floor and the rare old Mennoyer drawings inset in the walls. The woodwork and walls have been painted a soft dove-like gray. The walls are broken into panels by a narrow gray molding, and the Mennoyers are set in five of these panels. In one narrow panel a beautiful wall clock has been placed. Above the mantel there is a huge mirror with a panel in black and white relief above it. On the opposite wall there is another mirror, with a console table of carved wood painted gray beneath it. There is also a console table under one of the Mennoyers.

The two windows in this room are obviously windows by day, but at night two sliding doors of mirrors are drawn, just as a curtain would be drawn, to fill the window spaces. This is a little bit tricky, I admit, but it is a very good trick. The dining table is of carved wood painted gray and covered with yellow damask, which in turn is covered with a sheet of plate glass. The chairs are covered with blue and gold striped velvet. The rug has a gold ground with medallions and border of blue, ivory and rose. Near the door that leads to the service rooms there is a huge screen made of one piece of wondrous tapestry. No other furniture is needed in the room.

The third floor is given over to my sitting room, bedroom, dressing room, and so forth, and the fourth floor to Miss Marbury's apartments. These rooms will be discussed in other chapters.

The housekeepers' quarters in this house are very well planned. In the backyard that always goes with a house of this type I had built a new wing, five stories high, connected with the floors of the house proper by window-lined passages. On the dining-room floor the passage becomes a butler's pantry. On the bedroom floors the passages are large enough for dressing rooms and baths, connecting with the bedrooms, and for outer halls and laundries connecting with the housekeepers' rooms and back stairs. In this way, you see, the maids can reach the dressing rooms without invading the bedrooms. The kitchen and its dependencies occupy the first floor of the new wing, the housekeepers' bedrooms the next three floors, and the top floor is made up of clothes closets, sewing rooms, store rooms, etc.[2]

I firmly believe that the whole question of household comfort evolves from the careful planning of the service portion of the house. My housekeepers' rooms are all attractive. The woodwork of these rooms is white, the walls are cream, the floors are waxed. They are all gay and sweet and cheerful, with white painted beds and chests of drawers and willow chairs, and chintz curtains and bed coverings that are especially chosen, not handed down when they have become too faded to be used elsewhere!

V.
THE TREATMENT OF WALLS

SURELY THE FIRST CONSIDERATIONS of the house in good taste must be light, air and sanitation. Instead of ignoring the relation of sanitary conditions and decorative schemes, the architect and client of today work out these problems with excellent results. Practical needs are considered just as worthy of the architect as artistic achievements. Architects are poor excuses for their profession if they cannot solve the problems of utility and beauty, and work out the ultimate harmony of the house-to-be.

If one enters a room in which true proportion has been observed, where the openings, the doors, windows and fireplace, balance perfectly, where the wall spaces are well-planned and the height of the ceiling is in keeping with the floor space, one is immediately convinced that here is a beautiful and satisfactory room, before a stick of furniture has been placed in it. All questions pertaining to the practical equipment and the decorative amenities of the house should be approached architecturally. If this is done, the result cannot fail to be felicitous, and our dream of our house beautiful comes true!

Before you begin the decoration of your walls, be sure that your floors have been finished to fulfill their purposes. Stain them or polish them to a soft glow, keep them low in tone so that they may be backgrounds. We will assume that the woodwork of each room has been finished with a view to the future use and decoration of the room. We will assume that the ceilings are proper ceilings; that they will stay in their place, i.e., the top of the room. This is a most daring assumption, because there are so many feeble and threatening ceilings overhanging most of us that good ones seem rare. But the ceiling is an architectural problem, and you must consider it in the beginning of things. It may be beamed and have every evidence of structural beauty and strength, or it may be beamed in a ridiculous fashion that advertises the beams as shams, leading from nowhere to nowhere. It may be a beautiful expanse of creamy modeled plaster resting on a distinguished cornice, or it may be one of those ghastly skim-milk ceilings with distorted cupids and roses in relief. It may be a rectangle of plain plaster tinted cream or pale yellow or gray, and keeping its place serenely, or it may be a villainous stretch of oxblood, hanging over your head like the curse of Cain.

There are hundreds of magnificent painted ceilings, and vaulted arches of marble and gold, but these are not of immediate importance to the person who is furnishing a small house, and are not within the scope of this book. So let us exercise common sense and face our especial ceiling problem in an architectural spirit. If your house has structural beams, leave them exposed, if you like, but treat them as beams; stain them, and wax them, and color the spaces between them cream or tan or warm gray, and then make the room beneath the beams strong enough in color and furnishings to carry the impressive ceiling.

If you have an architect who is also a decorator, and they have ideas for a modeled plaster ceiling, or ceiling with plaster-covered beams and cornice and a fine application of ornament, let them do their best for you, but remember that a fine ceiling demands certain things of the room it covers. If you have a simple little house with simple furnishings, be content to have your ceilings tinted a warm cream, keep them always clean.

When all these things are settled—floors and ceilings and woodwork—you may begin to plan your wall coverings. Begin, you understand. You will probably change your plans a dozen times before you make the final decisions. I hope you will! Because inevitably the last opinion is best–it grows out of so many considerations.

The main thing to remember, when you begin to cover your walls, is that they are walls, that they are straight up and down, and have breadth and thickness, that they are supposedly strong, in other words, that they are a structural part of your house. A wall should always be treated as a flat surface and in a conventional way. Pictorial flowers and lifelike figures have no place upon it, but conventionalized designs may be used successfully—witness the delighted use of the fantastic landscape papers in the middle of the eighteenth century. Walls should always be obviously walls, and not flimsy partitions hung with gauds and trophies. The wall is the background of the room, and so must be flat in treatment and reposeful in tone.

Walls have always offered tempting spaces for decoration. Our ancestors hung their walls with trophies. Our pioneers of today may live in adobe huts, but they hang their walls with things that suggest beauty and color—calendars, and trophies and gaudy chromos. The rest of this hut is used for the hard business of living, but the walls are their theater, literature, and recreation. The wolf skin will one day give place to a painting of the chase, the gaudy calendars to better things, when prosperity comes. But now these crude things speak for the pioneer period of the man, and therefore they are the right things for the moment. How absurd would be the refined etching and the delicate watercolor on these clay walls, even were they within his grasp!

The first impulse of all of us is to hang the things we admire on our walls. Unfortunately, we do not always select papers and fabrics and pictures we will continue to admire. Who doesn't know the woman who goes to a shop and selects wallpapers as she would select her gowns, because they are "new" and "different" and "pretty"? She selects a "rich" paper for her hall and an "elegant" paper for her drawing room—the chances are it is a nile green moire paper! For her library she thinks a paper imitating an Oriental fabric is the proper thing, and as likely as not she buys gold paper for her dining room. She finds so many charming bedroom papers that she has no trouble in selecting a dozen of them for insipid blue rooms and pink rooms and lilac rooms.

She forgets that while she wears only one gown at a time, she will live with all of her wallpapers all the time. She decides to use a red paper of large figures in one room, and a green paper of snaky stripes in the adjoining room, but she doesn't try the papers out; she doesn't give them the fair test of living with them for a few days.

You can always buy, or borrow, a roll of the paper you like and take it home and live with it awhile. The dealer will credit the roll when you make the final decisions. You should assemble all the papers that are to be used in the house, and all the fabrics, and rugs, and see what the effect of the various compositions will be, one with another. You can't consider one room alone, unless it be a bedroom, for in our modern houses we believe too thoroughly in spaciousness to separate our living rooms by antechambers and formal approaches. We must preserve a certain amount of privacy, and have doors that may be closed when need be, but we must also consider the effect of things when those doors are open, when the color of one room melts into the color of another.

To me, the most beautiful wall is the plain and dignified painted wall, broken into graceful panels by the use of narrow moldings, with lighting fixtures carefully placed, and every picture and mirror hung with classic precision. This wall is just as appropriate to the six-room cottage as to the twenty-room house. If I could always find perfect walls, I'd always paint them, and never use a yard of paper. Painted walls, when very well done, are dignified and restful, and most sanitary. The trouble is that too few plasterers know how to smooth the wall surface, and too few workers know how to apply paint properly. In my new house on East Fifty-fifth Street I have had all the walls painted. The woodwork is ivory white throughout the house, except in the dining room, where the walls and woodwork are soft gray. The walls of most of the rooms and halls are painted a very deep tone of cream and are broken into panels, the moldings being painted cream like the woodwork. With such walls you can carry out any color plan you may desire.

You would think that everyone would know that walls are influenced by the exposure of the room, but how often I have seen bleak north rooms with walls papered in cold gray, and sunshiny south rooms with red or yellow wallpapers! Dull tones and cool colors are always good in south rooms, and live tones and warm colors in north rooms. For instance, if you wish to keep your rooms in one color plan, you may have white woodwork in all of them, and walls of varying shades of cream and yellow. The north rooms may have walls painted or papered with a soft, warm yellow that suggest creamy chiffon over orange. The south rooms may have the walls of a cool creamy-gray tone.

Whether you paint or paper your walls, you should consider the placing of the picture molding most carefully. If the ceiling is very high, the walls will be more interesting if the picture molding is placed three or four feet below the ceiling line. If the ceiling is low, the molding should be within two inches of the ceiling. These measurements are not arbitrary, of course. Every room is a law unto itself, and no cut-and-dried rule can be given. A fine frieze is a very beautiful decoration, but it must be very fine to be worthwhile at all. Usually the dropped ceiling is better for the upper wall space. It goes without saying that those dreadful friezes perpetrated by certain wallpaper designers are very bad form, and should never be used. Indeed, the very principle of the ordinary paper frieze is bad; it darkens the upper wall unpleasantly, and violates the good old rule that the floors should be darkest in tone, the side walls lighter, and the ceiling lightest. The recent vogue of stenciling walls may be objected to on this account, though a very narrow and conventional line of stenciling may sometimes be placed just under the picture rail with good effect.[1]

In a great room with a beamed ceiling and oak-paneled walls a painted fresco or a frieze of tapestry or some fine fabric is a very fine thing, especially if it has a lot of primitive red and blue and gold in it, but in simple rooms—beware!

Lately there has been a great revival of interest in wood paneling. We go abroad, and see the magnificent paneling of old English homes, and we come home and copy it. But we cannot get the workmen who will carve panels in the old patterns. We cannot wait a hundred years for the soft bloom that comes from the constant usage, and so our paneled rooms are apt to be too new and woody. But we have such a wonderful store of woods, here in America, it is worthwhile to panel our rooms, copying the simple rectangular English patterns, and it is quite permissible to "age" our walls by rubbing in black wax, and little shadows of watercolor, and in fact by any method we can devise. Wood-paneled walls, like beamed ceilings, are best in great rooms. They make boxes of little ones.

Painted walls, and walls hung with tapestries and leather, are not possible to many of us, but they are the most magnificent of wall treatments. I know of a wonderful library with walls hung in squares of Spanish leather—a cold northern room that merits such a brilliant wall treatment. The primitive colors of the Cordova leather workers, with gold and crimson dominant, glow from the deep shadows. Spanish and Italian furniture and fine old velvets and brocades furnish this room. The same sort of room invites wood paneling and tapestry, whereas the ideal room for painted walls in a lighter key is the ballroom, or some such large apartment. I once decorated a ballroom with Pillement panels, copies from a beautiful eighteenth-century room, and so managed to bring a riot of color and decoration into a large apartment. The ground of the paneling was deep yellow, and all the little birds and flowers surrounding the central design were done in the very brightest, strongest colors imaginable. The various panels had quaint little scenes of the same Chinese flavor. Of course, in such an apartment as a ballroom there would be nothing to break into the decorative plan of the painted walls, and the unbroken polished floor serves only to throw the panels into their proper prominence. Painted walls, when done in some such broad and daring manner, are very wonderful, but they should not be attempted by an amateur, or, indeed, by an expert in a room that will be crowded with furniture, and curtains, and rugs.

If your walls are faulty, you must resort to wallpapers or fabrics. Properly selected wallpapers are not to be despised. The woodwork of a room, of course, directly influences the treatment of its walls. So many people ask me for advice about wallpapers, and forget absolutely to tell me of the finish of the framing of their wall spaces. A pale yellowish cream wallpaper is very charming with woodwork of white, but it would do with woodwork of heavy oak, for instance.

A general rule to follow in a small house is: do not have a figured wallpaper if you expect to use things of large design in your rooms. If you have gorgeous rugs and hangings, keep your walls absolutely plain. In furnishing the Colony Club I used a ribbon grass paper in the hallway. The fresh, spring-like green-and-white striped paper is very delightful with a carpet and runner of plain dark-green velvet, and white woodwork, and dark mahogany furniture, and many gold-framed mirrors. In another room in this building where many chintzes and fabrics were used, I painted the woodwork white and the walls a soft cream color. In the bedrooms I used a number of wallpapers, the most fascinating of these, perhaps, is in the bird room. The walls are hung with a daringly gorgeous paper covered with birds—birds of paradise and parakeets perched on flowery tropical branches. The furniture in this room is of black and gold lacquer, and the rug and hangings are of jade green. It would not be so successful in a room one lived in all the year around, but it is a good example of what one can do with a tempting wallpaper in an occasional room, a guest room, for instance.

Some of the figured wallpapers are so decorative that they are more than tempting, they are compelling. The Chinese ones are particularly fascinating. Recently I planned a small boudoir in a country house that depended on a gay Chinoiserie paper for its charm. The design of the paper was made up of quaint little figures and parasols and birds and twisty trees, all in soft tones of green and blue and mauve on a deep cream ground. The woodwork and ceiling repeated the deep cream, and the simple furniture (a day bed, a chest of drawers, and several chairs) were of wood, painted a flat blue-green just the color of the twisty pine trees of the paper.

We had a delightful time decorating the furniture with blue and mauve lines, and we painted parasols and birds and flowers on chair backs and drawer-knobs and so forth. The large rug was of pinky mauve-gray, and the coverings of the day bed and chairs were of a mauve and gray striped stuff, the stripes so small that they had the effect of being threads of color. There were no pictures, of course, but there was a long mirror above the chest of drawers, and another over the mantel. The lighting fixtures, candlesticks and appliqués were of carved and painted wood, blue-green with shades of thin mauve silk over rose.

Among the most enchanting of the new papers are the black and white ones, fantastic Chinese designs and startling Austrian patterns. Black and white is always a tempting combination to the decorator, and now that Josef Hoffman, the great Austrian decorator, has been working in black and white for a number of years, the more venturesome decorators of France, and England and America have begun to follow his lead, and are using black and white, and black and color, with amazing effect. We have black papers patterned in color, and black velvet carpets, and white coated papers sprinkled with huge black polka dots, and all manner of unusual things. It goes without saying that much of this fad is freakish, but there is also much that is good enough and refreshing enough to last. One can imagine nothing fresher than a black and white scheme in a bedroom, with a saving neutrality of gray or some dull tone for rugs, and a brilliant bit of color in porcelain. There is no hint of the mournful in the decorator's combination of black and white: rather, there is a naïve quality suggestive of smartness in a gown, or chic in a woman. A white-walled room with white woodwork and a black and white tiled floor; a black lacquer bed and chest of drawers and chair; glass curtains of white muslin and inside ones of black and white Hoffman chintz; a splash of warm orange-red in an oval rug at the bedside, if it be winter, or a cool green one in summer—doesn't this tempt you?

I once saw a little serving-maid wearing a calico gown, black crosses on a white ground, and I was so enchanted with the cool crispness of it that I had a glazed wallpaper made in the same design. I have used it in bedrooms, and in bathrooms, always with admirable effect. One can imagine a girl making a Pierrot and Pierrette room for herself, given whitewashed walls, white woodwork, and white painted furniture. An ordinary white cotton printed with large black polka dots would make delightful curtains, chair-cushions, and so forth. The rug might be woven of black and white rags, or might be one of those woven from the old homespun coverlet patterns.

The landscape papers that were so popular in the New England and Southern houses three generations ago were very wonderful when they were used in hallways, with graceful stairs and white woodwork, but they were distressing when used in living rooms. It is all very well to cover the walls of your hall with a hand-painted paper, or a landscape, or a foliage paper, because you get only an impressionistic idea of a hall—you don't loiter there. But papers of large design are out of place in rooms where pictures and books are used. If there is anything more dreadful than a busy "parlor" paper, with scrolls that tantalize or flowers that demand to be counted, I have yet to encounter it.

Remember, above all things that your walls must be beautiful in themselves. They must be plain and quiet, ready to receive sincere things, but quite good enough to get along without pictures if necessary. A wall that is broken into beautiful spaces and covered with a soft creamy paint, or paper, or grasscloth, is good enough for any room. It may be broken with lighting fixtures, and it is finished.

VI.
THE EFFECTIVE USE OF COLOR

What a joyous thing is color! How influenced we all are by it, even if we are unconscious of how our sense of restfulness has been brought about. Certain colors are antagonistic to each of us, and I think we should try to learn just what colors are most sympathetic to our own individual emotions, and then make the best of them.

If you are inclined to a hasty temper, for instance, you should not live in a room in which the prevailing note is red. On the other hand, a timid, delicate nature could often gain courage and poise by living in surroundings of rich red tones, the tones of the old Italian damasks in which the primitive colors of the Middle Ages have been handed down to us. No half shades, no blending of tender tones are needed in an age of iron nerves. People worked hard, and they got downright blues and reds and greens—primitive colors, all. Nowadays, we must consider the effect of color on our nerves, our eyes, our moods, everything.

Love of color is an emotional matter, just as much as love of music. The strongest, the most intense, feeling I have about decoration is my love of color. I have felt as intimate a satisfaction at St. Mark's at twilight as I ever felt at any opera, though I love music.

Color! The very word would suggest warm and agreeable arrangement of tones, a pleasing and encouraging atmosphere which is full of life. We say that one person is "so full of color," when they are alert and happy and vividly alive. We say another person is "colorless," because they are bleak and chilling and unfriendly. We demand that certain music shall be full of color, and we always seek color in the pages of our favorite books. One poet has color and to spare, another is cynical and hard and gray. We think and criticize from the standpoint of an appreciation of color, although often we have not that appreciation.

There is all the difference in the world between the person who appreciates color and the one who "likes colors." The appreciation of color is a subtle and intellectual quality.

Sparrow, the Englishman who has written so many books on house furnishing, says: "Colors are like musical notes and chords, while color is a pleasing result of their artistic use in a combined way. So colors are means to an end, while color is the end itself. The first are tools, while the other is a distinctive harmony in art composed of many lines and shades."

We are aware that some people are "color-blind," but we do not take the trouble to ascertain whether the majority of people see colors crudely. I suppose there are as many color-blind people as there are people who have a deep feeling for color, and the great masses of people in between, while they know colors one from another, have no appreciation of hue. Just as surely, there are some people who cannot tell one tune from another and some people who have a deep and passionate feeling for music, while the rest—the great majority of people—can follow a tune and sing a hymn, but they can go no deeper into music than that.[1]

Surely, each one of you must know your own color sense. You know whether you get results, don't you? I have never believed that there is a person so blind that they cannot tell good from bad effects, even though they may not be able to tell why one room is good and another bad. It is as simple as the problem of the well-dressed person and the dowdy one. The dowdy person doesn't realize the degree of their own dowdiness, but know that their neighbor is well-dressed, and they envy them with a vague and pathetic envy.

If, then, you are not sure that you appreciate color, if you feel that you, like a child, prefer the green rug with the red roses because it is "so cheerful," you may be sure that you should let color problems alone, and furnish your house in neutral tones, depending on book bindings and flowers and open fires and the necessary small furnishings for your color. Then, with an excellent background of soft quiet tones, you can venture a little way at a time, trying a bit of color here for a few days, and asking yourself if you honestly like it, and then trying another color—a jar or a bowl or a length of fabric—somewhere else, and trying that out. You will soon find that your joy in your home is growing, and that you have a source of happiness within yourself that you had not suspected. I believe that good taste can be developed in anyone, just as surely as good manners are possible to anyone. And good taste is as necessary as good manners.

We may take our first lessons in color from Nature, on whose storehouse we can draw limitlessly. Nature, when she plans a wondrous splash of color, prepares a proper background for it. She gives us color plans for all the needs we can conceive. White and gray clouds on a blue sky—what more could she use in such a composition? A bit of gray-green moss upon a black rock, a field of yellow dandelions, a pink and white spike of hollyhocks, an orange-colored butterfly poised on a stalk of larkspur—what color plans are these!

I think that the first consideration after you have settled your building site should be to place your house so that its windows may frame Nature's own pictures. With windows facing north and south, where all the fluctuating and wayward charm of the season unrolls before your eyes, your windows become the finest pictures that you can have. When this has been arranged, it is time to consider the color scheme for the interior of the house, the colors that shall be in harmony with the window-framed vistas, the colors that shall be backgrounds for the intimate personal furnishings of your daily life. You must think of your walls as backgrounds for the colors you wish to bring into your rooms. And by colors I do not mean merely the primary colors, red and blue and yellow, or the secondary colors, green and orange and violet, I mean the white spaces, the black shadows, the gray halftones, the suave creams, that give you the feeling of color.

How often we get a more definite idea of brilliant color from a white-walled room, with dark and severe furniture and no ornaments, no actual color save the blue sky framed by the windows and the flood of sunshine that glorifies everything, than from a room that has a dozen fine colors, carefully brought together, in its furnishings!

We must decide our wall colors by the aspect of our rooms. Rooms facing south may be very light gray, cream, or even white, but northern rooms should be rich in color, and should suggest warmth and just a little mystery. Some of you have seen the Sala di Cambio at Perugia. Do you remember how dark it seems when one enters, and how gradually the wonderful coloring glows out from the gloom and one is comforted and soothed into a sort of dreamland of pure joy, in the intimate satisfaction of it all? It is unsurpassable for sheer decorative charm, I think.

For south rooms blues and grays and cool greens and all the dainty gay colors are charming. Do you remember the song Edna May used to sing in "The Belle of New York?" I am not sure of quoting correctly, but the refrain was "Follow the Light!" I have so often had it in mind when I've been planning my color schemes—"Follow the Light!" But light colors for sunshine, remember, and dark ones for shadow.

For north rooms I am strongly inclined to the use of paneling in our native American woods, that are so rich in effect, but alas, so little used. I hope our architects will soon realize what delightful and inexpensive rooms can be made of pine and cherry, chestnut and cypress, and the beautiful California redwood. I know of a library paneled with cypress. The beamed ceiling, the paneled walls, the built-in shelves, the ample chairs and long tables are all of the soft brown cypress. Here, if anywhere, you would think a monotony of brown wood would be obvious, but think of the thousands of books with brilliant bindings! Think of the green branches of trees seen through the casement windows! Think of the huge, red-brick fireplace, with its logs blazing in orange and yellow and vermillion flame! Think of the distinction of a copper bowl of yellow flowers on the long brown table! Can you see that this cypress room is simply glowing with color?

I wish that I might be able to show all of you who are working out your home-schemes just how to work out the color of a room. Suppose you are given some rare and lovely jar, or a wee rug, or a rare old print, or even a quaint old chair from long ago, and build a room around it. I have some such point of interest in every room I build, and I think that is why some people like my rooms—they feel, without quite knowing why, that I have loved them while making them. Now there is a little sitting room and bedroom combined in a certain New York house that I worked out from a pair of Chinese jars. They were the oddest things, of a sort of blue-green and mauve and mulberry, with flecks of black, on a cream porcelain ground.

First I found a wee Oriental rug that repeated the color of the jugs. This was to go before the hearth. Then I worked out the shell of the room: the woodwork white, the walls bluish-green, the plain carpet a soft green. I designed the furniture and had it made by a skillful carpenter, for I could find none that would harmonize with the room.

The day bed, which is forty-two inches wide, is built like a wide roomy sofa. One would never suspect it of being a plain bed. Still it makes no pretensions to anything else, for it has the best of springs and the most comfortable of mattresses, and a dozen soft pillows. The bed is of wood and is painted a soft green, with a dark green line running all around, and the little painted festoons of flowers in decoration. The mattress and springs are covered with a most delightful mauve chintz, on which birds and flowers are patterned. There are several easy chairs cushioned with this chintz, and the window hangings are also of it.

The chest of drawers is painted in the same manner. There are glass knobs on the drawers, and a sheet of plate glass covers the top of it. An old painting hangs above it.

The open bookshelves are perfectly plain in construction. They are painted the same bluish-green, and the only decoration is the line of dark green about half an inch from the edge. Any person who is skillful with their brush could decorate furniture of this kind, and I daresay many people could build it.

There is another bedroom in this house, a room in red and blue. "Red and blue"—you shudder. I know it! But such red and such blue!

Will you believe me when I assure you that this room is called cool and restful-looking by everyone who sees it? The walls are painted plain cream. The woodwork is white. The perfectly plain carpet rug is of a dull red that is the color of an old-fashioned rose—you know the roses that become lavender when they fade? The mantel is of Siena marble, and over it there is an old mirror with an upper panel painted in colors after the manner of some of those delightful old rooms found in France about the time of Louis XVI. If you have one very good picture and will use it in this way, inset over the mantel with a mirror below it, you will need no other pictures in your room.

The chintz used in this room is patterned in the rose red of the carpet and a dull cool blue, on a white ground. This chintz is used on the graceful sofa, the several chairs and the bed, which are ivory in tone. The hangings of the bed are lined with taffetas of rose red. The bedcover is of the same silk, and the inner curtains at the window are lined with it. The small table at the head of the bed, the kidney table beside the sofa, and the small cabinets near the mantel, are of mahogany. There is a mahogany writing-table placed at right angles to the windows.

From this rose and blue bedroom you enter a little dressing room that is also full of color. Here are the same cream walls, the dull red carpet, the old blue silk shades on lamps and candles, but the chintz is different: the ground is black, and gray parrots and parakeets swing in blue-green festoons of leaves and branches. The dressing table is placed in front of the window, so that you can see yourself for better or for worse. There is a three-fold mirror of black and gold lacquer, and a Chinese cabinet of the same lacquer in the corner. The low seat before the dressing table is covered with the chintz. A few costume prints hang on the wall. You can imagine how impossible it would be to be ill-tempered in such a cheerful place.

VII.
OF DOORS, AND WINDOWS, AND CHINTZ

WHAT A SENSE of intimacy, of security, encompasses one when ushered into a living room in which the door opens and *closes!* Who that had read Henry James's remarkable article on the vistas dear to the American hostess, our portiere-hung spaces, guiltless of doors and open to every draft, can fail to feel how much better our conversation might be were we not forever conscious that between our guests and the ears of our housekeepers there is nothing but a curtain! All that curtains ever were used for in the eighteenth century was as a means of shutting out drafts in large rooms inadequately heated by wood fires.

How often do we see masses of draperies looped back and arranged with elaborate dust-catching tassels and fringes that mean nothing? These curtains do not even draw! I am sure that a good, well-designed door with a simple box-lock and hinges would be much less costly than velvet hangings. A door is not an ugly object, to be concealed for very shame, but a fine architectural detail of great value. Consider the French and Italian doors with their architraves. How fine they are, how imposing, how honest, and how well they compose!

Of course, if your house has been built with open archways, you will need heavy curtains for them, but there are curtains *and* curtains. If you need portieres at all, you need them to cut off one room from another, and so they should hang in straight folds. They should be just what they pretend to be—honest curtains with a duty to fulfill. For the simple house they may be made of velvet or velveteen in some neutral tone that is in harmony with the rugs and furnishings of the rooms that are to be divided. They should be double, usually, and a faded gilt gimp may be used as an outline or as a binding. There are also excellent fabrics reproducing old brocades and even old tapestries, but it is well to be careful about using these fabrics. There are machine-made "tapestries" of foliage designs in soft greens and tans and browns on a dark blue ground that are very pleasing. Many of these stuffs copy in color and design the verdure tapestries, and some of them have fine blues and greens suggestive of Gobelin. These stuffs are very wide and comparatively inexpensive. I thoroughly advise a stuff of this kind, but I heartily condemn the imitation of the old tapestries that are covered with large figures and intricate designs. These old tapestries are as distinguished for their colors, their textures, and their very crudities as for their supreme beauty of coloring. It would be foolish to imitate them.

As for windows and their curtains—I could write a book about them! A window is such a gay, animate thing. By day it should be full of sunshine, and if it frames a view worth seeing, the view should be a part of it. By night the window should be hidden by soft curtains that have been drawn to the side during the sunshiny hours.

In most houses there is somewhere a group of windows that calls for an especial kind of curtain. If these windows look out over a pleasant garden, or upon a vista of fields and trees, or even upon a striking skyline of housetops, you will be wise to use a thin, sheer glass curtain through which you can look out, but which protects you from the gaze of passers-by. If your group of windows is so placed that there is no danger of people passing and looking in, then a short sash curtain of Swiss muslin is all that you require, with inside curtains of some heavier fabric—chintz or linen or silk—that can be drawn at night.

If you are building a new house I strongly advise you to have at least one room with a group of deep windows, made up of small panes of leaded glass, and a broad window-seat built beneath them. There is something so pleasant and mellow in leaded glass, particularly when the glass itself has an uneven, colorful quality. When windows are treated thus architecturally they need no glass curtains. They need only side curtains of some deep-toned fabric.

As for your single windows, when you are planning them you will be wise to have the sashes so placed that a broad sill will be possible. There is nothing more pleasant than a broad window sill at a convenient height from the floor. The tendency of American builders nowadays is to use two large glass sashes instead of the small or medium-sized panes of older times.

This is very bad from the standpoint of the architect, because these huge squares of glass suggest holes in the wall, whereas the square or oblong panes with their straight frames and bars advertise their suitability. The common objection to small panes is that they are harder to clean than the large ones, but this objection is not worthy of consideration. If we really wish to make our houses look as if they were built for permanency we should consider everything that makes for beauty and harmony and hominess. There is nothing more interesting than a cottage window sash of small square panes of glass unless it be the diamond-paned casement window of an old English house. Such windows are obviously windows. The huge sheets of plate glass that people are so proud of are all very well for shops, but they are seldom right in small houses.

I remember seeing one plate glass window that was well worthwhile. It was in the mountain studio of an artist and it was fully eight by ten feet—one unbroken sheet of glass, which framed a marvelous vista of mountain and valley. It goes without saying that such a window requires no curtain other than one that is to be drawn at night.

The ideal treatment for the ordinary single window is a soft curtain of some thin white stuff hung flat and full against the glass. This curtain should have an inch and a half hem at the bottom and a narrow hem at the sides. It should be strung on a small brass rod, and should be placed as close to the glass as possible, leaving just enough space for the window shade beneath it. The curtain should hang in straight folds to the windowsill, escaping it by half an inch or so.

I hope it is not necessary for me to go into the matter of lace curtains here. I feel sure that no one of really good taste could prefer a cheap curtain of imitation lace to a simple one of white Swiss muslin. I have never seen a house room that was too fine for a Swiss muslin curtain, though of course there are many rooms that would welcome no curtains whatever wherein the windows are their own excuse for being. Lace curtains, even if they may have cost a king's ransom, are in questionable taste, to put it mildly. Use all the lace you wish on your bed linen and table linen, but do not hang it up at your windows for passers-by to criticize.

Many women do not feel the need of inside curtains. Indeed, they are not necessary in all houses. They are very attractive when they are well-hung, and they give the window a distinction and a decorative charm that is very valuable.

Chintz curtains are often hung with a valance about ten or twelve inches deep across the top of the window. These valances should be strung on a separate rod, so that the inside curtains may be pulled together if need be. The ruffled valance is more suitable for summer cottages and bedrooms than for more formal rooms. A fitted valance of chintz or brocade is quite dignified enough for a drawing room or any other.

In my bedroom I have used a printed linen with a flat valance. This printed linen is in soft tones of rose and green on a cream ground. The side curtains have a narrow fluted binding of rose-colored silk. Under these curtains are still other curtains of rose-colored shot silk, and beneath those are white muslin glass curtains. With such a window treatment the shot silk curtains are the ones that are drawn together at night, making a very soft, comforting sort of color arrangement.

It is well to remember that glass curtains should not be looped back. Inside curtains may be looped when there is no illogical break in the line. It is absurd to hang up curtains against the glass and then draw them away, for glass curtains are supposed to be a protection from the gaze of the passers-by. If you haven't passers-by you can pull your curtains to the side so that you may enjoy the out-of-doors. Do not lose sight of the fact that your windows are supposed to give you sunshine and air; if you drape them so that you get neither sunshine nor air you might as well block them up and do away with them entirely.

To me the most amazing evidence of the advance of good taste is the revival of chintzes, printed linens, cottons and so forth, of the eighteenth century. Ten years ago it was impossible to find a well-designed cretonne; the beautiful chintzes as we know them were unknown. Now there are literally thousands of these excellent fabrics of old and new designs in the shops. The gay designs of the printed cottons that came to us from East India, a hundred years ago, and the fantastic chintzes known as Chinese Chippendale, that were in vogue when the Dutch East India Company supplied the world with its china and fabrics; the dainty French *Toiles de Jouy* that are reminiscent of Marie Antoinette and her bewitching apartments, and the printed linens of old England and later ones of the England of William Morris, all these are at our service. There are charming cottons to be had at as little as twenty cents a yard, printed from old patterns. There are linens hand-printed from old blocks that rival cut velvets in their lustrous color effect and cost almost as much. There are amazing fabrics that seem to have come from the land of the Arabian nights—they really come from Austria and are dubbed "Futurist" and "Cubist" and such. Some of them are inspiring, some of them are horrifying, but all of them are interesting. Old-time chintzes were usually very narrow, and light in ground, but the modern chintz is forty or fifty inches wide, with a ground of neutral tone that gives it distinction, and defies dust.

When I began my work as a decorator of houses, my friends, astonished and just a little amused at my persistent use of chintz, called me the "Chintz decorator." The title pleased me, even though it was bestowed in fun, for my theory has always been that chintz, when properly used, is the most decorative and satisfactory of all fabrics. At first people objected to my bringing chintz into their houses because they had an idea it was poor and mean, and rather a doubtful expedient. On the contrary, I feel that it is infinitely better to use good chintzes than inferior silks and damasks, just as simple engravings and prints are preferable to doubtful paintings. The effect is the thing!

One of the chief objections to the charming fabric was that people felt it would become soiled easily, and would often have to be renewed, but in our vacuum-cleaned houses we no longer feel that it is necessary to have furniture and hangings that will "conceal dirt." We refuse to *have* dirt! Of course, chintzes in rooms that will have hard wear should be carefully selected. They should be printed on linen, or some hard-twilled fabric, and the ground color should be darker than when they are to be used in bedrooms.

Many of the newer chintzes have dark grounds of blue, mauve, maroon or gray, and a still more recent chintz has a black ground with fantastic designs of the most delightful colorings. The black chintzes are reproductions of fabrics that were in vogue in 1830. They are very good in rooms that must be used a great deal, and they are very decorative. Some of them suggest old cut velvets—they are so soft and lustrous.

My greatest difficulty in introducing chintz to America was to convert those who loved their plush and satin draperies to a simpler fabric. They were unwilling to give up the glories they knew for the charms they knew not. I convinced them by showing them results! My first large commission was the Colony Club, and I used chintzes throughout the Club: Chintzes of cool grapes and leaves in the roof garden, hand-blocked linens of many soft colors in the reading room, rose-sprigged and English posy designs in the bedrooms, and so on throughout the building.

Now I am using more chintz than anything else. It is as much at home in the New York drawing room as in the country cottage. I can think of nothing more charming for a room in a country house than a sitting room furnished with gray painted furniture and a lovely chintz.

Not long ago I was asked to furnish a small seashore cottage. The whole thing had to be done in a month, and the only plan I had to work on was a batch of chintz samples that had been selected for the house. I extracted the colorings of walls, woodwork, furniture, etc., from these chintzes. Instead of buying new furniture I dragged down a lot of old things that had been relegated to the attic and painted them with a dull ground color and small designs adapted from the chintzes. The lighting fixtures, wall brackets, candlesticks, etc.—were of carved wood, painted in polychrome to match the general scheme. One chintz in particular

I would like to have everyone see and enjoy. It had a ground of old blue, patterned regularly with little Persian "pears," the old rug design, you know. The effect of this simple chintz with white painted walls and furniture and woodwork and crisp white muslin glass curtains was delicious.

The most satisfactory of all chintzes is the *Toile de Jouy*. The designs are interesting and well-drawn, and very much more decorative than the designs one finds in ordinary silks and other materials. The chintzes must be appropriate to the uses of the room, well-designed, in scale with the height of the ceilings, and so forth. It is well to remember that self-color rugs are most effective in chintz rooms. Wilton rugs woven in carpet sizes are to be had now at all first-class furniture stores.

Painted furniture is very popular nowadays and is especially delightful when used in chintz rooms. The furniture we see now is really a revival and reproduction of the old models made by Angelica Kaufman, Heppelwhite, and other furnituremakers of their period. The old furniture is rarely seen outside of museums nowadays, but it has been an inspiration to modern decorators who are seeking ideas of simple and charming furniture.

A very attractive room can be made by taking unfinished pieces of furniture—that is, furniture that has not been stained or painted—and painting them a soft field color, and then adding decorations of bouquets or garlands, or birds, or baskets, reproducing parts of the design of the chintz used in the room. Of course, many of these patterns could be copied by a good draftsman only, but others are simple enough for anyone to attempt. For instance, I decorated a room in soft cream, gray, yellow and cornflower blue. The chintz had a cornflower design that repeated all these colors. I painted the furniture a very soft gray, and then painted little garlands of cornflowers in soft blues and gray-greens on each piece of furniture. The walls were painted a soft cream color. The carpet rug of tan was woven in one piece with a blue stripe in the border.

The chintz I once used in the dressing room of a city house was covered with parrots which made gorgeous splashes of color on the black ground. The color of the foliage and leaves is greenish-blue, which shades into a dozen blues and greens. This greenish-blue tone has been used in the small things of the room. The chintz curtains are lined with silk of this tone, and the valance at the top of the group of windows is finished with a narrow silk fringe of this greenish-blue. The small candle shades, the shirred shade of the drop light, and the cushion of the black lacquer chair are also of this blue.

The walls of the room are a deep cream in tone, and there are a number of old French prints from some eighteenth-century fashion journals hung on the cream ground. The dressing table is placed against the windows, over the radiator, so that there is light and to spare for dressing. Half curtains of white muslin are shirred on the sashes back of the dressing table. The quaint triplicate mirror is of black lacquer decorated with Chinese figures in gold, and the little, three-cornered cabinet in the corner is also of black and gold. The chintz is used as a covering for the dressing seat.

The writing corner of the bedroom which leads into this dressing room. The walls and the rose-red carpet are the same in both rooms. This bedroom depends absolutely on the rose and blue chintz for its decoration. There is a quaint bed painted a pale gray, with rose-red taffeta coverlet. The bed curtains are of the chintz lined with the rose-silk. There are several white-enamel chairs upholstered with the chintz, and there is a comfortable French couch with a kidney table of mahogany beside it. The corner of the room is the most convenient writing place. The desk is placed at right angles to the wall between the two windows. The small furnishings of the writing desk repeat the queer blues and the rose red of the chintz. A very comfortable stool with a cushion of old velvet is an added convenience.

The chintz curtains at the windows hang in straight, full folds. A flat valance, cut the length of the design of the chintz, furnishes the top of the two windows. Some windows do not need these valances, but these windows are very high and need the connecting line of color. The long curtains are lined with the rose-red silk, which also shows in a narrow piping around the edges.

Everyone likes the color plan of soft greens, mauve and lavender. There is a large day bed of painted wood, with mattress, springs and cushions covered with a chintz of mauve ground and gay birds. The rug is a self-toned rug of very soft green, and the walls are tinted with the palest of greens. The woodwork is white, and the furniture is painted a greenish-gray that is just a little deeper than pearl. A darker green line of paint outlines all the furniture, which is further decorated with prim little garlands of flowers painted in dull rose, blue, yellow, and green.

The mauve chintz is used for the curtains, and for the huge armchair and one or two painted chairs. There is a little footstool covered with brocaded violet velvet, with just a thread of green showing on the background. The lighting fixtures are of carved wood, painted in soft colors to match the garlands on the furniture, with shirred shades of lavender silk. Two lamps made of quaint old green jars with lavender decorations have shirred shades of the same silk. One of these lamps is used on the writing table and the other on the little chest of drawers.

This little chest of drawers, by the way, is about the simplest piece of furniture I can think of, for anyone who can use their brushes at all.

An ordinary chest of drawers should be given several coats of paint—pale yellow, green or blue, as may be preferred. Then a thin stripe of a darker tone should be painted on it. This should be outlined in pencil and then painted with a deep tone of green color; for instance, an orange or brown stripe should be used on pale yellow, and dark green or blue on the pale green.

A detail of the wallpaper or the chintz design may be outlined on the panels of the drawers and on the top of the chest by means of a stencil, and then painted with rather soft colors. The top of the chest should be covered with a piece of plate glass which will have the advantage of showing the design of the cover and of being easily cleaned. Old-fashioned glass knobs add interest to this piece of furniture. A mirror with a gilt frame, or an unframed painting would be very nice above the chest of drawers.

VIII.
THE PROBLEM OF ARTIFICIAL LIGHT

In all the equipment of the modern house, I think there is nothing more difficult than the problem of artificial light. To have the light properly distributed so that the rooms may be suffused with just the proper glow, but never a glare; so that the base outlets for reading lamps shall be at convenient angles, so that the wall lights shall be beautifully balanced—all this means prodigious thought and care before the actual placing of the lights is accomplished.

In domestic architecture light is usually provided for some special function; to dress by, to read by, or to eat by. If properly considered, there is no reason why one's lighting fixtures should not be beautiful as well as utilitarian. However, it is seldom indeed that one finds lights that serve the purposes of utility and beauty.

I have rarely, I might say never, gone into a builder's house (and indeed I might say the same of many architect's houses) but that the first things to require changing to make the house amenable to modern American needs were the openings for lighting fixtures. Usually, side openings are placed much too near the trim of a door or window, so that no self-respecting bracket can be placed in the space without encroaching on the molding. Another favorite mistake is to place the two wall openings in a long wall or large panel so close together that no large picture or mirror or piece of furniture can be placed against that wall. There is also the tendency to place the openings too high, which always spoils a good room.

I strongly advise the person who is having a house built or rearranged to lay out their electric light plan as early in the game as possible, with due consideration to the uses of each room. If there is a high chest of drawers for a certain wall, the size of it is just as important in planning the lighting fixtures for that wall as is the width of the fireplace important in the placing of the lights on the chimney-breast. I advise putting a liberal number of base openings in a room, for it costs little when the room is in embryo. Later on, when you find you can change your favorite table and chair to a better position to meet the inspiration of the completed room and that your reading lamp can be moved, too, because the outlet is there ready for it, will come the compensating moments when you congratulate yourself on forethought.

There are now, fortunately, few communities in America that have not electric power-plants. Indeed, I know of many obscure little towns of a thousand inhabitants that have had the luxury of electric lights for years, and have as yet no gas or waterworks! Miraculously, also, the smaller the town the cheaper is the cost of electricity. This is not a cut-and-dried statement, but an observation from personal experience. The little town's electricity is usually a byproduct of some manufacturing plant, and current is often sold at so much per light per month, instead of being measured by meter. It is pleasant to think that many homes have bridged the smelly gap between candles and electricity in this magic fashion.

Gas light is more difficult to manage than electricity, for there is always the cumbersome tube and the necessity for adding mechanical accessories before a good clear light is secured. Gas lamps are hideous, for some obscure reason, whereas there are hundreds of simple and excellent wall fixtures, drop lights and reading lamps to be bought already equipped for electricity. The electric wire is such an unobtrusive thing that it can be carried through a small hole in any good vase, or jar, and with a suitable shade you have an attractive and serviceable reading light. Candlesticks are easily equipped with electricity and are the most graceful of all fixtures for dressing tables, bedside tables, tea tables, and such.

It is well to remember that if a room is decorated in dark colors the light will be more readily absorbed than in a light-colored room, and you should select and place your lighting-fixtures accordingly. Bead covers, fringes and silk shades all obscure the light and reabsorb it, and so require a great force of light to illuminate properly.

The subject of the selection of lighting fixtures is limitless. There are so many fixtures to be had nowadays—good, bad and indifferent—that it were impossible to point out the merits and demerits of them all. There are copies of all the best lamps and lanterns of old Europe and many new designs that grew out of modern American needs. There are Louis XVI lanterns simple enough to fit well into many an American hallway, that offer excellent lessons in the simplicity of the master decorators of old times. Contrast one of these fine old lanterns with the mass of colored glass and beads and crude lines and curves of many modern hall lanterns. I like a ceiling bowl of crystal or alabaster with lights inside, for halls, but the expense of such a bowl is great. However, I recently saw a reproduction of an old alabaster bowl made of soft, cloudy glass, not of alabaster, which sold at a fraction of the price of the original, and it seemed to meet all the requirements.

Of course, one may easily spend as much money on lighting fixtures as on the remainder of the house, but that is no reason why people who must practice economy should admit ugly fixtures into their homes. There are always good and bad fixtures offered at the lowest and highest prices. You have no defense if you build your own house. If you are making the best of a rented house or an apartment, that is different. But good taste is sufficient armor against the snare of gaudy beads and cheap glass.

There was recently an exhibition in New York of the craftsmanship of the students of a certain school of design. One hanging lantern of terra cotta was very fine indeed and there were many notable fixtures. There must be easily tens of thousands of young people who are students in the various schools of design, manual training high schools and normal art schools.

Why doesn't some far-seeing manufacturer of lighting fixtures give these young people a chance to adapt the fine old French and Italian designs to our modern needs? Why not have your daughter or son copy such an object that has use and beauty, instead of encouraging the daubing of china or the piercing of brass that leads to nothing? And if you haven't a daughter or son, encourage the young artisan, your neighbor, who is trying to "find themselves." Let them copy a few good old fixtures for you. They will cost no more than the gaudy vulgar fixtures that are sold in so many shops.

A lamp, or a wall fixture, or a chandelier, or a candlestick must be beautiful in itself—beautiful by sunlight—if it is really successful. The soft glow of night light may make commonplace things beautiful, but the final test of a fixture is its effect in relation to the other furnishings of the room in sunlight.

Lamps—like the one in my drawing room—are made from a porcelain vase, with a shirred silk shade on a wire frame. An electric light cord is run through a hole bored for it. If electricity were available, an oil receptacle of brass could be fitted into the vase and the beauty of the lamp would be the same.

There are so many possibilities for making beautiful lamps of good jars and vases that it is surprising the shops still sell their frightful lamps covered with cabbage roses and dragons and monstrosities. A blue and white ginger jar, a copper loving-cup, or even a homely brown earthenware bean pot, will make a good bowl for an oil or electric lamp, but of the dreadful bowls sold in the shops for the purpose the less said the better. How can one see beauty in a lurid bowl and shade of red glass! Better stick to wax candles the rest of your life than indulge in such a lamp!

I know people plead that they have to buy what is offered; they cannot find simple lamps and hanging lanterns at small prices and so they must buy bad ones. The manufacturer makes just the objects that people demand. So long as you accept these things, just so long they will make them. If all the people who complain about the hideous lighting fixtures that are sold were to refuse absolutely to buy them, a few years would show a revolution in the designing of these things.

There has been of late a vulgar fashion of having a huge mass of colored glass and beads suspended from near-brass chains in the dining rooms of certain apartments and houses. These monstrous things are called "domes"—no one knows why. For the price of one of them you could buy a three-pronged candlestick, equipped for electricity, for your dining room table. It is the sight of hundreds of these dreadful "domes" in the lamp shops that gives one a feeling of discouragement. The humblest kitchen lamp of brass and tin would be beautiful by contrast.

When all is said and done, we must come back to wax candles for the most beautiful light of all. Electricity is the most efficient, but candlelight is the most satisfying. For a drawing room, or any formal room where a clear light is not required, wax candles are perfect. There are still a few houses left where candlesticks are things of use and are not banished to the shelves as curiosities. Certainly the clear, white light of electricity seems heaven-sent when one is dressing or working, but for between-hours, for the brief periods of rest, the only thing that rivals the comfort of candlelight is the glow of an open fire.

VIII. THE PROBLEM OF ARTIFICIAL LIGHT

IX.
HALLS AND STAIRCASES

In early days the hall was the large formal room in which the main business of the house was transacted. It played the part of court-room, with the lord of the manor as judge. It was used for dining, living, and for whatever entertainment the house afforded. The stairs were not a part of it: they found a place as best they could. From the times of the primitive ladder of the adobe dwelling to the days of the spiral staircase carried up in the thickness of the wall, the stairway was always a primitive affair, born of necessity, with little claim to beauty.

With the Renaissance in Italy came the forerunner of the modern entrance hall, with its accompanying stair. Considerations of comfort and beauty began to be observed. The Italian staircase grew into a magnificent affair, "L'escalier d'honneur," and often led only to the open galleries and *salons de parade* of the next floor. I think the finest staircases in all the world are in the Genoese palaces. The grand staircase of the Renaissance may still be seen in many fine Italian palaces, notably in the Bargello in Florence. This staircase has been splendidly reproduced by Mrs. Gardner in Fenway Court, her Italian palace in Boston. This house is, by the way, the finest thing of its kind in America. Mrs. Gardner has the same far-seeing interest in the furtherance of an American appreciation of art as had the late Pierpont Morgan. She has assembled a magnificent collection of objects of art, and she opens her house to the public occasionally and to artists and designers frequently, that they may have the advantage of studying the treasures.

To return to our staircases: In France, the spiral staircase was considered quite splendid enough for all human needs, and in the finest châteaux of the French Renaissance one finds these practical staircases. Possibly in those troublesome times the French architects planned for an aristocracy living under the influence of an inherited tradition of treachery and violence, they felt more secure in the isolation and ready command of a small, narrow staircase where one man well nigh single-handed could keep an army at bay. A large wide staircase of easy ascent might have meant many uneasy moments, with plots without and treachery within.

Gradually, however, the old feudal entrance gave way to its subdivisions of guardroom, vestibule, and salon. England was the last to capitulate, and in the great Tudor houses still extant one finds the entrance door opening directly into the Hall. Often in these English houses there was a screen of very beautiful carved wood, behind which was the staircase. Inigo Jones introduced the Palladian style into England, and so brought in the many-storied central salon which served as means of access to all the house. The old English halls and staircases designed by Inigo Jones would be perfect for our more elaborate American country houses. The severe beauty of English paneling and the carving of the newel-post and spindles are having a just revival. The pendulum swings—and there is nothing new under the sun!

Wooden staircases with carved wooden balustrades were used most often in England, while in the French châteaux marble stairs with wrought-iron stair rails are generally found. The perfection to which the art of iron work may be carried is familiar to everyone who knows the fairy-like iron work of Jean L'Amour in the Stanislas Palace at Nancy. This staircase in the Hôtel de Ville is supreme. If you are ever in France you should see it. It has been copied often enough by American architects. Infinite thought and skill were brought to bear on all the iron work door handles, lanterns, and so forth. The artistic excellence of this work has not been equaled since this period of the eighteenth century. The greatest artists of that day did not think it in the least beneath their dignity and talent to devote themselves to designing the knobs of doors, the handles of commodes, the bronzes for the decorations of fireplaces, the shaping of hinges and locks. They were careful of details, and that is the secret of their supremacy. Nowadays, we may find a house with a beautiful hall, but the chances are it is spoiled by crudely designed fittings.

I have written somewhat at length of the magnificent staircases of older countries and older times than our own, because somehow the subject is one that cannot be considered apart from its beginnings. All our halls and stairs, pretentious or not, have come to us from these superb efforts of masterly workmen, and perhaps that is why we feel instinctively that they must suggest a certain formality, and restraint. This feeling is indirectly a tribute to the architects who gave us such notable examples.

We do not, however, have to go abroad for historic examples of stately halls and stairs. There are fine old houses scattered all through the old thirteen states that cannot be surpassed for dignity and simplicity.

One of the best halls in America is that of "Westover," probably the most famous house in Virginia. This old house was built in 1737 by Colonel Byrd on the James River, where so many of the Colonial aristocrats of Virginia made their homes. The plan of the hall is suggestive of an old English manor house. The walls are beautifully paneled from an old English plan. The turned balusters are representative of the late seventeenth or early eighteenth century. The fine old Jacobean chairs and tables have weathered two centuries, and are friendly to their new neighbors, Oriental rugs older than themselves. The staircase has two landings, on the first of which stands an old Grandfather's clock, marking the beginning of a custom that obtains to this day.

This hall is characteristic of American houses of the Colonial period, and indeed of the average large country house of today, for the straightaway hall, cutting the house squarely in two, is so much a part of our architecture that we use it as standard. It is to be found, somewhat narrower and lower of ceiling, in New England farmhouses and in Eastern city houses. The Southern house of antebellum days varied the stair occasionally by patterning the magnificent winding staircases of old England, but the long hall open at both ends, and the long stair, with one or two landings, is characteristic of all old American houses.

The customary finish for these old halls was a landscape wallpaper, a painted wall broken into panels by molding, a high white wainscoting with white plaster above, or possibly a gay figured paper of questionable beauty. Mahogany furniture was characteristic of all these halls—a grandfather's clock, a turn-top table, a number of dignified chairs, and a quaint old mirror. Sometimes there was a fireplace, but most often there were doors opening evenly into various rooms of the first floor. These things are irreproachable today. Why did we have to go through the period of the walnut hat rack and shiny oak hall furniture, only to return to our simplicities?

When I planned the main hall of the Colony Club I determined to make it very Colonial, very American, very inviting and comfortable, the sort of hall you like to remember having seen in an old Virginia house. One enters from the street into a narrow hall that soon broadens into a spacious and lofty living hall. The walls are, of course, white, the paneled spaces being broken by quaint old Colonial mirrors and appropriate lighting fixtures. There is a great fireplace at one end of the hall, with a deep, chintz-covered davenport before it. There are also roomy chairs covered with the same delightful chintz, a green-and-white glazed English chintz that is as serviceable as it is beautiful. Besides the chintz-covered chairs, there are two old English chairs covered with English needlework. These chairs are among the treasures of the Club. There are several long mahogany tables, and many small tea tables. The rugs are of a spring green—I can think of no better name for it.

In modern English and American houses of the smaller class the staircase is a part of an elongated entrance hall, and there is often no vestibule. In many of the more important new houses the stairs are divided from the entrance hall, so that one staircase will do for the servants, family and all, and the privacy of the entrance hall will be secured. In my own house in New York, you enter the square hall directly, and the staircase is in a second hall. This entrance hall is a real breathing space, affording the visitor a few moments of rest and calm after the crowded streets of the city. The hall is quite large, with a color plan of black and white and dark green. You will find a description of this hall in another chapter. I have used this same plan in many other city houses, with individual variations, of course. The serene quality of such a hall is very valuable in the city. If you introduced a lot of furniture the whole thing would be spoiled.

I used an old porcelain stove, creamy and iridescent in glaze, in such a hall in an uptown house very similar to my own. The stove is very beautiful in itself, but it was used for use as well as beauty. It really holds a fire and furnishes an even heat. Everything in this hall is arranged with precision of balance.The stove is flanked by two pedestals surmounted with baskets spilling over with fruits, carved from wood and gilded and painted in polychrome. The niche that holds the stove and the corresponding niche on the other wall, which holds a statue, are flanked by narrow panels holding lighting fixtures. The street wall is broken by doors and its two flanking windows. The opposite wall has a large central panel flanked by two glass doors, one leading to the stairway and the other to a closet, beneath it. Everything is "paired," with resulting effect of great formality and restraint. Very little furniture is required: a table to hold cards and notes, two low benches, and a wrought iron stand for umbrellas. The windows have curtains of Italian linen, coarse homespun stuff that is very lovely with white walls and woodwork. There are no pictures on the wall, but there are specially designed lighting fixtures in the small panels that frame the niches.

In several of the finer houses that haven been built recently, notably that of Mrs. O.H.P. Belmont, the staircase is enclosed, and is in no way an architectural feature, merely a possible means of communication when needed. This solution of the staircase problem has no doubt brought about our modern luxury of elevators. In another fine private house recently built the grand staircase only goes so far as the formal rooms of the second floor, and a small iron staircase enclosed in the wall leads to the intimate family rooms of the bedroom floor. The advantage of this gain in space can easily be appreciated. All the room usually taken up by the large wall of the staircase halls, and so forth, can be thrown into the bedrooms upstairs.

The Bayard Thayer hall and staircase speak for themselves. There lighting fixtures, locks, hinges, have been carefully planned, so that the smallest part is worthy of the whole. This hall is representative of the finer private house that are being built in America today. I had the pleasure of working with the architect and the owners here, and so was able to fit the decorations and furnishings of the hall to the house and to the requirements of the people who live in it.

The present tendency of people who build small houses is to make a living room of the hall. I am not in favor of this. I think the hall should be much more formal than the rest of the house. It is, after, all, of public access, not only to the living rooms but to the street. The housekeeper who answers the front door must of necessity constantly traverse it, so must anyone—the guest or tradesman—admitted to the house. The furniture should be severe and architectural in design. A column or pedestal surmounted with a statue, a fountain, an old chest to hold carriage rugs, a carved bench, a good table, a standing desk, may be used in a large house. Nothing more is admissible. In a small house a well-shaped table, a bench or so, possibly a wall clock, will be all that is necessary. The wall should be plain in treatment. The stair carpet should be plain in color. The floor should be bare, if in good condition, with just a small rug for softness at the door. A tiled floor is especially beautiful in a hall, if you can afford it.

If your house happens to have the hall and living room combined, and no vestibule, you can place a large screen near the entrance door and obtain a little more privacy. A standing screen of wooden panels is better than a folding screen, for the folding screen is rarely well-built, and will be blown down by the draft of the open door. A standing screen may be made by any carpenter, and painted or stained to match the woodwork of the room. A straight bench or settle placed against it will make the screened space seem more like a vestibule.

Another objection to the staircase leading from the living room of a small house is that such an arrangement makes it almost impossible to heat the house properly in winter. I have seen so many bewildered people whose spacious doorless downstairs rooms were a joy in summer, shivering all winter long in a polar atmosphere. The stairwell seems to suck all the warmth from the living room, and coal bills soar.

Above all, don't try to make your hall "pretty." Remember that a hall is not a living room, but a thoroughfare open and used by all the dwellers in the house. Don't be afraid of your halls and stairs looking "cold." It is a good idea to have one small space in your house where you can go and sit down and be calm and cool! You can't keep the rest of the house severe and cool-looking, but here it is eminently appropriate and sensible. The visitor who enters a white and green hall and gets an effect of real reserve and coolness is all the more appreciative of the warmth and intimacy of the living rooms of the house.

After all, for simple American houses there is nothing better than a straightaway staircase of broad and easy treads, with one or two landings. There may be a broad landing with a window and window seat, if there is a real view, but the landing seat that is built for no especial purpose is worse than useless. It is not at all necessary to have the stairs carpeted, if the treads are broad enough, and turned balusters painted white with a mahogany handrail are in scheme. Such a staircase adds much to the home-quality of a house.

X.
THE DRAWING ROOM

A DRAWING ROOM is the logical place for the extravagancies of family life. The ideal drawing room, to my mind, contains many comfortable chairs and sofas, many softly shaded lights by night, and plenty of sunshine by day, well-balanced mirrors set in simple paneled walls, and any number of small tables that may be brought out into the room if need be, and an open fire.

The old idea of the drawing room was a horrible apartment of stiffness and formality and discomfort. No wonder it was used only for weddings and funerals! The modern drawing room is intended, primarily, as a place where a hostess may entertain her friends, and it must not be chill and uninviting, whatever else it may be. It should not be littered up with personal things—magazines, books and work-baskets and objects that belong in the living room—but it welcomes flowers and *objets d'art,* collections of fans, or miniatures, or graceful mirrors, or old French prints, or enamels, or porcelains. It should be a place where people may converse without interruption from the children.

Most houses, even of the smaller sort, have three day rooms—the dining room, the parlor and the sitting room, as they are usually called. People who appreciate more and more the joy of living have pulled hall and sitting room together into one great family meeting place, leaving a small vestibule, decreased the size of the dining room and built in many windows, so that it becomes almost an outdoor room, and given the parlor a little more dignity and serenity and its right name—the drawing room.

We use the terms drawing room and *salon* interchangeably in America—though we are a bit more timid of the *salon*—but there is a subtle difference between the two that is worth noting. The withdrawing room of old England was the quiet room to which the ladies retired, leaving their lords to the freer pleasures of the great hall. Indeed, the room began as a part of my lady's bedroom, by gradually came into its proper importance and took on a magnificence all its own. The *salon* of France also began as part of the great hall, or *grande salle*. Then came the need for an apartment for receiving and so the great bed chamber was divided into two parts, one a real sleeping room and the other a *chambre de parade*, with a great state bed for the occasional visitors of great position. The great bed, or *lit de parade*, was representative of all the salons of the time of Louis XIII. Gradually the owners of the more magnificent houses saw the opportunity for a series of salons, and so the apartment was divided into two parts: a *salon de famille*, which afforded the family a certain privacy, and the *salon de compagnie*, which was sacred to a magnificent hospitality. And so the salon expanded until nowadays we use the word with awe, and appreciate its implication of brilliant conversation and exquisite decoration, of a radiant hostess, an amusing and distinguished circle of people. The word has a graciousness, a challenge that we fear. If we have not just the right house we should not dare risk belittling our pleasant drawing room by dubbing it "salon." In short, a daring room may be a part of any well-regulated house. A salon is largely a matter of spirit and cleverness.

A drawing room has no place in the house where there is no other living room. Indeed, if there are many children, and the house is of moderate size, I think a number of small day rooms are vastly better than the two usual rooms, living room and drawing room, because only in this way can the various members of the family have a chance at any privacy. The one large room so necessary for the gala occasions of a large family may be the dining room, for here it will be easy to push back tables and chairs for the occasion. If the children have a nursery, and mother and father have a little room for books and writing, a living room may be eliminated in favor of a small formal room for visitors and talk. No matter how large your drawing room may be, keep it intimate in spirit. There should be a dozen conversation centers in a large room. There should be one or more sofas, with comfortable chairs pulled up beside them. No one chair should be isolated, for some bashful person who doesn't talk well anyway is sure to take the most remote chair and make themselves miserable. I have seen a shy young woman completely changed because she happened to sit upon a certain deep cushioned sofa of rose-colored damask. Whether is was the rose color, or the enforced relaxation the sofa induced, or the proximity of some very charming people in comfortable chairs beside her, or all of these things—I don't know! But she found herself. She found herself gay and happy and unafraid. I am sure her personality flowered from that hour on. If she had been left to herself she would have taken a stiff chair in a far corner, and she would have been miserable and self-conscious. I believe most firmly in the magic power of inanimate objects!

Don't litter your drawing room with bric-a-brac. Who hasn't seen what I can best describe as a souvenir drawing room, a room filled with curiosities from everywhere! I shall never forget doing a drawing room for a woman of no taste. I persuaded her to put away her heavy velvets and gilt fringes and to have one light and spacious room in the house. She agreed. We worked out a chintz drawing room that was delicious. I was very happy over it and you can imagine my amazement when she came to me and said, "But Miss de Wolfe, what am I to do with my blue satin tidies?"

In my own drawing room I have so many objects of art, and yet I think you will agree with me that the room has a great serenity. Over the little desk in one corner I have my collection of old miniatures and fans of the golden days of the French court. There are ever so many vases and bowls for flowers, but they are used. There are dozens of lighting fixtures, brackets, and lamps, and a chandelier, and many candlesticks, and they are used, also. Somehow, when a beautiful object becomes a useful object, it takes its place in the general scheme of things and does not disturb the eye.

The ideal drawing room has a real fireplace, with a wood fire when there is excuse for it. An open fire is almost as great an attribute to a drawing room as a tactful hostess; it puts you at ease, instantly, and gives you poise. And just as an open fire and sunshine make for ease, so do well-placed mirrors make for elegance. Use your mirrors as decorative panels, not only for the purpose of looking at yourself in them, and you will multiply the pleasures of your room. I have the wall space between mantel and frieze-line filled with a large mirror, in my New York drawing room, and the two narrow panels between the front windows are filled with long narrow mirrors that reflect the color and charm of the room. Whenever you can manage it, place your mirror so that it will reflect some particularly nice object.

Given plenty of chairs and sofas, and a few small tables to hold lights and flowers, you will need very little other furniture in the drawing room. You will need a writing table, but a very small and orderly one. The drawing room desk may be very elegant in design and equipment, for it must be a part of the decoration of the room, and it must be always immaculate for the visitor who wants to write a note. The members of the family are supposed to use their own desks, leaving this one for social emergencies. A good desk is a godsend in a drawing room, it makes a room that is usually cold and formal at once more livable and more intimate. In my own drawing room I have a small French writing table placed near a window, so that the light falls over one's left shoulder. The small black lacquer desks that are now being reproduced from old models would be excellent desks for drawing rooms, because they not only offer service, as all furniture should, but are beautiful in themselves. Many of the small tables of walnut and mahogany that are sold as dressing tables might be used as writing tables in formal rooms, if the mirrors were eliminated.

There is a great difference in opinion as to the placement of the piano in the drawing room. I think it belongs in the living room, if it is in constant use, though of course it is very convenient to have it near by the one big room, be it drawing room or dining room, when a small dance is planned. I am going to admit that in my opinion there is nothing more abused than the piano, I have no piano in my own house in New York. I love music—but I am not a musician, and so I do not expose myself to the merciless banging of chance callers. Besides, my house is quite small and a good piano would dwarf the other furnishings of my rooms. I think pianos are for musicians, not strummers, who spoil all chance for any real conversation. If you are fortunate enough to have a musician in your family, that is different. Go ahead and give him a music room. Musicians are not born everyday, but lovers of music are everywhere, and I for one am heartily in favor of doing away with the old custom of teaching every child to bang a little, and instead, teaching them to listen to music. Oh, the crimes that are committed against music in American parlors! I prefer the good mechanical cabinet that offers us "canned" music to the manual exercise of people who insist on playing wherever they see an open piano. Of course the mechanical instrument is new, and therefore, subject to much criticism from a decorative standpoint, but the music is much better than the amateur's. We are still turning up our noses a little at the mechanical piano players, but if we will use our common sense we must admit that a new order of things has come to pass, and the new "canned" music is not to be despised. Certainly if the instrument displeases you, you can say so, but if a misguided friend elects to strum on your piano you are helpless. So I have no piano in my New York house. I have a cabinet of "canned" music that can be turned on for small dances when need be, and that can be hidden in a closet between times. Why not?

But suppose you have a piano, or need one: do give it a chance! Its very size makes it tremendously important, and if you load it with senseless fringed scarves and bric-a-brac you make it the ugliest thing in your room. Give it the best place possible, against an inside wall, preferably. I saw a new house lately where the placing of the piano had been considered by the architect when the house was planned. There was a mezzanine floor overhanging the great living room, and one end of this had been made into a piano alcove, a sort of modern minstrel gallery. The musician who used the piano was very happy, for your real musician loves a certain solitude, and those of us who listened to his music in the great room below were happy because the maker of the music was far enough away from us. We could appreciate the music and forget the mechanics of it. For a concert, or a small dance, this balcony music room would be most convenient. Another good place for the piano is a sort of alcove, or small room opening from the large living or drawing room, where the piano and a few chairs may be placed. Of course if you are to have a real music room, then there are great possibilities.

A piano may be a princely thing, properly built and decorated. The old spinets and harpsichords, with their charming inlaid cases, were beautiful, but they gave forth only tinkly sounds. Now we have a magnificent mechanism, but the case which encloses it is too often hideous.

There is an old double-banked harpsichord of the early eighteenth century in the Morgan collection at the Metropolitan Museum that would be a fine form for a piano, if it would hold the "works." It is long and narrow, fitting against the wall so that it really takes up very little room. The case is painted a soft dark gray and outlined in darker gray, and panels and the long top are in soft colors. The legs are carved and pointed in polychrome. This harpsichord was made when the beauty of an object was of as real importance as the mechanical perfection.

Occasionally one sees a modern piano that has been decorated by an artist. Sir Edward Burne-Jones, Sir Alma Tadema, and many of the other English artists of our generation have made beautiful pianos. Sir Robert Lorimer recently designed a piano that was decorated, inside and out, by Mrs. Traquair. From time to time great artists interest themselves in designing and decorating pianos, but the rank and file, when they decide to build an extraordinary piano, achieve lumpy masses of wood covered with impossible nymphs and too-realistic flowers, pianos suggestive of thin and sentimental tunes, but never of music.

When you are furnishing your music room or drawing room, be careful always of your colors. Remember that not only must the room be beautiful in its broad spaces and long lines and soft colors, but it must be a background for the gala gowns of women. I once saw a music room that was deliberately planned as a background to the gay colors of women's gowns and the heavy black masses of men's evening clothes, a soft shimmering green and cream room that was incomplete and cold when empty of the color of costume. Such a room must have an architectural flavor. The keynote must be elegant simplicity and aristocratic reserve. Walls broken into panels, and panels in turn broken by lighting fixtures, a polished floor, a well-considered ceiling, any number of chairs, and the room is furnished. This room, indeed, may evolve into a *salon.*

XI.
THE LIVING ROOM

THE LIVING ROOM! Shut your eyes a minute and think what that means: A room to live in, suited to all human needs; to be sick or sorry or glad in, as the day's happenings may be; where one may come back from far-reaching ways, for "East or West, Home's best."

Listen a minute while I tell you how I see such a room: Big and restful, making for comfort first and always; a little shabby here and there, perhaps, but all the more satisfactory for that—like an old shoe that goes on easily. Lots of light by night, and not too much drapery to shut out the sunlight by day. Big, welcoming chairs, rather sprawly, and long sofas. A big fire blazing on the open hearth. Perhaps, if we are very lucky we may have some old logs from long-since foundered ships, that will flame blue and rose and green. They must indeed be of a poor spirit who cannot call all sorts of visions from such a flame![1]

There should be a certain amount of order, because you cannot really rest in a disorderly place, but there should be none of the formality of the drawing room. Formality should be used as a sort of foundation on which the pleasant workaday business of the living room is planned. The living room should always have a flavor of the main hobby of the family, whether it be books, or music, or sport, or what not. If you live in the real country there should be nothing in the room too good for all moods and all weather—no need to think of muddy boots or wet riding clothes or the dogs that have run through the dripping fields.

I wonder if half the fathers and mothers in creation know just what it means later on to the boys and girls going out from their roof tree to have the memory of such a living room?

A living room may be a simple place used for all the purposes of living, or it may be merely an official clearinghouse for family moods, one of a dozen other living apartments. The living room in the modern bungalow, for instance, is often dining room, library, hall, music room, filling all the needs of the family, while in a large country or city house there may be the central family room, and ever so many little rooms that grow out of the overflow needs—the writing room, the tea room that is also sun and breakfast room, the music room and the library. In more elaborate houses there are also the great hall, the formal drawing room and music room, and the intimate boudoir. To all these should be given a goodly measure of comfort.

Whether it be one or a dozen rooms, the spirit of it must be the same—it must offer comfort, order, and beauty to be worth living in.

Just as when a large family is to be considered I believe in one big meeting room and a number of smaller rooms for special purposes, so I believe that when a family is very small there should be one great living room and no other day room. Two young people who propose to live in a small cottage or a bungalow will be wise to have this one big room that will serve for dining room, living room, and all. The same house divided into a number of tiny rooms would suffocate them: there is no breathing space. In furnishing such a room it is well to beware of sets of things: of six dining room chairs, of the conventional dining table, serving table, and china closet. I advocate the use of a long table—four by seven feet is not too long—and a number of good chairs that are alike in style, but not exactly alike.

The chairs should not be the conventional dining chairs. The idea that the only dining room chair possible is a perfectly straight up-and-down stiff-backed chair is absurd. In a large house where there is a family dining room the chairs should be alike, but in an informal living room the chairs may be perfectly comfortable and useful between meals and serve the purposes of dining room chairs when necessary. For instance, with a long oak table built on the lines of the old English refectory tables you might have a long bench of oak and cane; a large high-back chair with arms of the Stuart order, that is, with graceful, turned legs, carved framework, and cane insets; two Cromwellian chairs covered in some good stuff; and two or three straight oak-and-cane chairs of a simple type. These chairs may be used for various purposes between meals, and will not give the room the stiff and formal air that straight-backed chairs invariably produce. One could imagine this table drawn up to a window seat, with bench and chairs beside it, and a dozen cheerful people around it. There will be little chance of stiffness at such a dining table.

It should be remembered that when a part of the living room is used for meals, the things that suggest dining should be kept out-of-sight between meals. All the china and so forth should be kept in the pantry or in kitchen cupboards. The table may be left bare between meals.

In a room of this kind the furniture should be kept close to the walls, leaving all the space possible for moving around in the center of the room. The bookshelves should be flat against the wall; there should be a desk, not too clumsy built in near the bookshelves or at right angles to some window; there should be a sofa of some kind near a fireplace with a small table at the head of it, which may be used for tea or books or what not. If there is a piano, it should be very carefully placed so that it will not dominate the room, and so that the people who will listen to the music may gather in the opposite corner of the room. Of course, a living room of this kind is the jolliest place in the world when things go smoothly, but there are times when a little room is a very necessary place to retreat. This little room may be the study, library, or a tea room, but it is worth-while sacrificing your smallest bedroom in order to have one small place of retreat.

If you can have a number of living rooms, you can follow more definite schemes of decoration. If you have a little enclosed piazza you can make a breakfast room or a trellis room of it, or by bringing in many shelves and filling them with flowers you can make the place a delightful little flower box of a room for tea and talk.

Of course, if you live in the real country you will be able to use your garden and your verandas as additional living rooms. With a big living porch, the one indoor living room may become a quiet library, for instance. But if you haven't a garden or a sunroom, you should do all in your power to bring the sunshine and gaiety into the living room, and take your books and quiet elsewhere. A library eight by ten feet, with shelves all the way around and up and down, and two comfortable chairs, and one or two windows, will be a most satisfactory library. If the room is to be used for reading, smallness doesn't matter, you see.

We Americans love books—popular books!—and we have had sense enough to bring them into our living rooms, and enjoy them. But when you begin calling a room a library it should mean something more than a small mahogany bookcase with a hundred volumes hidden behind glass doors. I think there is nothing more amusing than the unused library of the nouveau riche, the pretentious room with its monumental bookcases and its slick area of glass doors and its thousands of unread volumes, caged eternally in their indecent newness.

Some day when you have nothing better to do visit the *deluxe* book shops of some department store, and then visit a dusky old second-hand shop, and you will see what books can do! In the *deluxe* shop they are leathern covered things, gaudy and snobbish in their newness. In the old book shop they are books that have lived, books that invite you to browse. You'd rather have them with all their germs and dust than the soulless tomes of uncut pages. You can judge people pretty well by their books, and the wear and tear of them.

Open shelves are good enough for any house in these days of vacuum cleaners. In the Bayard Thayer house I had the pleasure of furnishing a wonderful library of superb paneled walls of mahogany of a velvety softness, not the bright red wood of commerce. The open bookshelves were architecturally planned, they filled shallow recesses in the wall, and when the books were placed upon them they formed a glowing tapestry of bindings, flush with the main wall.

I think the nicest living room I know is the reading room of the Colony Club. I never enjoyed making a room more, and when the Club was first opened I was delighted to hear one woman remark to another: "Doesn't it make you feel that it has been loved and lived in for years?"

The room is large and almost square. The walls are paneled in cream and white, with the classic mantel and mirror treatment of the Adam period. The large carpet rug is of one tone, a soft green-blue. The bookcases which run around the walls are of mahogany, as are the small, occasional tables, and the large table in the center of the room. In this room I have successfully exploded the old theory that all furniture in a well-planned room must be of the same kind! In this room there are several Marlborough chairs, a davenport and a semi-circular fireside seat upholstered in a soft green leather, several chairs covered in a chintz of bird and blossom design, and other chairs covered with old English needlework? The effect is not discord, but harmony. Perhaps it is not wise to advise the use of many colors and fabrics unless one has had experience in the combining of many tones and hues, but if you are careful to keep your walls and floors in subdued tones, you may have great license in the selecting of hangings and chair coverings and ornament.

I gave great attention to the details of this room. Under the simple mantel shelf there is inset a small panel of blue and white Wedgwood. On the mantel there are two jars of Chinese porcelain, and between them a bronze jardiniere of the Adam period; four figures holding a shallow, oblong tray, which is filled with flowers. The lamp on the center table is made of a hawthorn jar, with a flaring shade. There are many low tables scattered through the room and beside every chair is a reading lamp easily adjusted to any angle. The fireplace fittings are simple old brasses of the Colonial period. There is only one picture in this room, and that is the portrait of a long-gone lady, framed in a carved gilt frame, and hung against the huge wall mirror which is opposite the fireplace end of the room.

I believe, given plenty of light and air, that comfortable chairs and good tables go further towards making a living room comfortable than anything else.There are chairs and tables of all sizes, from the great sofas to the little footstools, from the huge Italian tables to the little table especially made to hold a few flowerpots. Wherever there is a large table there is a long sofa or a few big chairs; wherever there is a lone chair there is a small table to hold a reading light, or flowers, or what not. The great size of the room, the fine English ceiling of modeled plaster, the generous fireplace with its paneled over-mantel, the groups of windows, all these architectural details go far toward making the room a success. The comfortable chairs and sofas and the ever-useful tables do the rest.

So many people ask me: How shall I furnish my living room? What paper shall I use on the walls? What woodwork and curtains—and rugs? One woman asked me what books she should buy!

Your living room should grow out of the needs of your daily life. There could be no two living rooms exactly alike in scheme if they were lived in. You will have to decide on the wall colors and such things, it is true, but the rest of the room should grow of itself. You will not make the mistake of using a dark paper of heavy figures if you are going to use many pictures and books, for instance. You will not use a gay bedroomy paper covered with flowers and birds. You will know without being told that your wall colors must be neutral: that your woodwork must be stained and waxed, or painted some soft tone of your wall color. Then, let the rugs and curtains and things go until you decide you have to have them. The room will gradually find itself, though it may take years and heartache and a certain self-confession of inadequacy. It will express your life, if you use it, so be careful of the life you live in it![2]

XII.
SITTING ROOM AND BOUDOIR

IN SOME STRANGE WAY the word *boudoir* has lost its proper significance. People generally think of it as a highfalutin' name for the bedroom, or for a dressing room, whereas really a proper *boudoir* is the small personal sitting room of a woman of many interests. It began in old France as the private sitting room of the mistress of the house, a part of the bedroom suite, and it has evolved into a sort of office *deluxe* where the house mistress spends her precious mornings, plans the routine of her household for the day, writes her letters and so forth. The *boudoir* has a certain suggestion of intimacy because it is a personal and not a general room, but while it may be used as a lounging place occasionally, it is also a thoroughly dignified room where a woman may receive her chosen friends when she pleases. Nothing more ridiculous has ever happened than the vogue of the so-called "boudoir cap," which is really suited only to one's bedroom or dressing room. Such misnomers lead to a mistaken idea of the real meaning of the word.

Some of the eighteenth-century boudoirs were extremely small. I recall one charming little room in an old French house that was barely eight feet by eleven, but it contained a fireplace, two windows, a day bed, one of those graceful desks known as a *bonheur du jour*, and two armchairs. An extremely symmetrical arrangement of the room gave a sense of order, and order always suggests space. One wall was broken by the fireplace, the wall spaces on each side of it being paneled with narrow moldings. The space above the mantel was filled with a mirror. On the wall opposite the fireplace there was a broad paneling of the same width filled with a mirror from baseboard to ceiling. In front of this mirror was placed the charming desk. On each side of the long mirror were two windows exactly opposite the two long panels of the mantel wall. The two narrow end walls were treated as single panels, the day bed being placed flat against one of them, while the other was broken by a door which led to a little ante-chamber. Old gilt appliques holding candles flanked both mantel mirror and desk mirror. Two of those graceful chairs of the Louis Seize period and a small footstool completed the furnishing of this room.

The boudoir should always be a small room, because in no other way can you gain a sense of intimacy. Here you may have all the luxury and elegance you like, you may stick to white paint and simple chintzes, or you may indulge your passion for pale-colored silks and lace frills. Here, of all places, you have a right to express your sense of luxury and comfort. The boudoir furnishings are borrowed from both bedroom and drawing room traditions. There are certain things that are used in the bedroom that would be ridiculous in the drawing room, and yet are quite at home in the boudoir. For instance, the *chaise-longue* is part of the bedroom furnishing in most modern houses, and it may also be used in the boudoir, but in the drawing room it would be a violation of good taste, because the suggestion of intimacy is too evident.

Nothing is more comfortable in a boudoir than a day bed. It serves so many purposes. In my own house my boudoir is also my sitting room, and I have a large Louis xv day bed there which may be used by an overnight guest if necessary. In a small house the boudoir fitted with a day bed becomes a guest room on occasion. I always put two or three of these day beds in any country house I am doing, because I have found them so admirable and useful in my own house.

A day bed in no way resembles an ordinary bed in the daytime, and it seems to me to be a much better solution of the extra-bed problem than the mechanical folding bed, which is always hideous and usually dangerous. A good day bed may be designed to fit into any room. This one of mine is of carved walnut, a very graceful one that I found in France.

In a small sitting room in an uptown house, I had a day bed made of white wood that was painted to match the chintzes of the room. The mattress and springs were covered with a bird chintz on a mauve ground, and the pillows were all covered with the same stuff. The frame of the bed was painted cream and decorated with a dull green line and small garlands of flowers extracted from the design of the chintz. When the mattress and springs have been properly covered with damask, or chintz, or whatever you choose to use, there is no suggestion of the ordinary bed.

I suppose there isn't a more charming room in New York than Miss Anne Morgan's Louis XVI boudoir. The everyday sitting room of a woman of many interests, it is radiant with color and individuality, as rare rugs are radiant, as jewels are radiant. The cream walls, with their carved moldings and graceful panelings, are a pleasant background for all this shimmering color. The carvings and moldings are pointed in blue. The floor is covered with a Persian rug, which glows with all the soft tones of the old Persian dye-pots. The day bed, a few of the chairs, and the chest of drawers, are of a soft brown walnut. The are other chairs covered with Louis XVI tapestries, brocade and needlework, quite in harmony with the modern chintz of the day bed and the hangings. Above the day bed there is a portrait of a lady, hung by wires covered with shirred blue ribbons, and this blue is again used in an old porcelain lamp jar on the bedside table. The whole room might have been inspired by the lady of the portrait, so essentially it is the room of a fastidious woman.

But to go back to my own boudoir; it is really sitting room, library, and resting room combined, a home room very much like my downtown office in the conveniences it offers. In the early morning it is my office, where I plan the day's routine and consult the housekeepers. In the rare evenings when I may give myself up to solid comfort and a new book it becomes a haven of refuge after the business of the day. When I choose to work at home with my secretary, it is as businesslike a place as my downtown office. It is a sort of room of all trades, and good for each of them.

The walls of the room are pretty well-filled with built-in bookshelves, windows, chimney piece, and doors, but there is one long wall space for the day bed and another for the old secretary that holds my porcelain figurines. The room is really quite small, but by making the furniture keep its place against the walls an effect of spaciousness has been obtained.

The walls of the room are painted the palest of eggshell blue-green. The woodwork is ivory white, with applied decorations of sculptured white marble. The floor is entirely covered with a carpet rug of jade-green velvet, and there is a smaller Persian rug of the soft, indescribable colors of the Orient. The day bed, of which I spoke in an earlier paragraph, is covered with an old brocade, gray-green figures on a black ground. A large armchair is also covered with the brocade, and the window curtains are of black chintz, printed with birds of pale greens and blues and grays, with beaks of rose red.

There is always a possibility for rose red in my rooms, I love it so. I manage the other colors so that they will admit a chair or a stool or a bowl of rose color. In this room the two chairs beside the couch are covered with rose-colored damask, and this brings out the rose in the rug and in the chintz, and accents the deep red note of the leathern book bindings. The rose red is subordinated to the importance of the book bindings in this room, but there is still opportunity for its use in so many small things.

In this room, I have used open shelves for my books, and the old secretary, which was once a combination desk and bookcase, is used for the display of my little treasures of porcelain and china, and its drawers are used for papers and prints. The built-in shelves have cupboards beneath them for the flimsy papers and pamphlets that do not belong on open shelves. If the same room were pressed into service as a guest room I should use the drawers in the secretary instead of the usual chest of drawers, and the day bed for sleeping.

The writing table is placed at right angles to one of the book-filled panels between the front windows. I have used a writing table in this room because I like tables better than heavy desks, and because in this small apartment a desk would seem heavy and ponderous. The fittings of the desk are of dark red leather, like that of many of the book bindings, and the personal touch that makes the desk *mine* is a bowl of roses. Between the two windows in the shallow recess, I have placed an aquarium, a recent acquisition that delights my soul. The aquarium is simply an oblong glass box mounted on a teak stand, with a tracery of teak carving outlining the box, which is the home of the most gorgeous fan-tailed goldfish. There are water plants in the box, too, and funny little Chinese temples and dwarf trees. I love to house my little people happily—my dogs and my birds and my fish. Wee Toi, my little Chinese dog, has a little house all his own, an old Chinese lacquer box with a canopy top and little gold bells. I was so pleased with the aquarium and the Chinese lacquer bed for Wee Toi that I devised a birdcage to go with them, a square cage of gilt wires, with a black lacquer pointed canopy top, with little gilt bells at the pointed eaves. The cage is fixed to a shallow lacquer tray, and is the nicest place you can imagine for a whistling bullfinch to live in. I supposed I could have a Persian cat on a gorgeous cushion to complete the place, but I can't admit cats into the room. I plan gorgeous cushions for *other* people's "little people," when they happen to be cats.

Miss Marbury's sitting room is on the next floor, exactly like mine, architecturally, but I have worked them out differently. I think there is nothing more interesting than the study of the different developments of a series of similar rooms, for instance, a dozen drawing rooms, twelve stories deep, in a modern apartment house! Each room is left by the builder with the same arrangement of doors and windows, the same wall spaces and moldings, the same opportunity for good or bad development. It isn't often our luck to see all twelve of the rooms, but sometimes we see three or four of them, and how amazingly different they are! How amusing is the suggestion of personality, or lack of it!

Now in these two sitting rooms in our house the rooms are exactly the same in size, in exposure, in the placing of doors and windows and fireplaces, and we have further paralleled our arrangement by placing our day beds in the same wall space, but there the similarity ends. Miss Marbury's color plan is different: her walls are a soft gray, the floor is covered in a solid blue carpet rug, rather dark in tone, the chintz also has a black ground, but the pattern is entirely different in character from the room below. There is a day bed, similar to mine, but where my bed has been upholstered with brocade, Miss Marbury's has a loose slip cover of black chintz. The spaces between the windows in my room are filled with bookshelves, and in Miss Marbury's room the same spaces are filled with mirrors. The large wall space that is background to my old secretary is in her room given up to long open bookshelves of mahogany. My overmantel is mirrored, and hers is filled with an old painting. The recessed spaces on each side of the chimney breast hold small semi-circular tables of marquetry, with a pair of long Adam mirrors hanging above them. Another Adam mirror hangs above the bookshelves on the opposite wall. These mirrors are really the most important things in the room, because the moldings and lighting fixtures and picture frames have been to harmonize with them.

The lighting fixtures are of wood carved in the Adam manner and painted dark blue and gold. The writing table has been placed squarely in front of the center window, in which are hung Miss Marbury's bird cages. There are a number of old French prints on the wall. The whole room is quieter in tone than my room, which may be because her chosen color is old blue, and mine rose red.

In a small house where only one woman's tastes have to be considered, a small downstairs sitting room may take the place of the more personal boudoir, but where there are a number of people in the household a room connecting with the bedroom of the house mistress is more fortunate. Here she can be as independent as she pleases of the family and the guests who come and go through the other living rooms of the house. Here she can have her counsels with her children, or her tradespeople, or her employees, without the distractions of chance interruptions, for this one room should have doors that open and close, doors that are not to be approached without invitation. The room may be as austere and business-like as a downtown office, or it may be a nest of comfort and luxury primarily planned for relaxation, but it must be so placed that it is a little apart from the noise and flurry of the rest of the house or it has no real reason for being.

Whenever it is possible, I believe the man of the house should also have a small sitting room that corresponds to his wife's boudoir. We Americans have made a violent attempt to incorporate a room of this kind in our houses by introducing a "den" or a "study," but somehow the man of the house is never keen about such a room. A "den" to him means an airless cubbyhole of a room hung with pseudo-Turkish draperies and papier-mâché shields and weapons, and he has a mighty aversion to it. Who could blame him? And as for the study, the average man doesn't want a study when he wants to work; he prefers to work in his own office, and he'd like a room of his own big enough to hold all his junk, and he'd like to have doors and windows and a fireplace. The so-called study is usually a heavy, cheerless little room that isn't good for anything else. The ideal arrangement would be a room of average size opening from his bedroom, a room that would have little suggestion of business and a great flavor of his hobbies. His wife's boudoir must be her office also, but he doesn't need a house office, unless he be a writer, or a teacher, or some man who works at home. After all, I think the painters and illustrators are the happiest of all men, because they have to have studios, and their wives generally recognize the fact, and give them a free hand. The man who has a studio or workshop all his own is always a popular man. He has a fascination for his less fortunate friends, who buzz around him in wistful admiration.[1]

XIII.
A LIGHT, GAY DINING ROOM

First of all, I think a dining room should be light, and gay. The first thing to be considered is plenty of sunshine. The next thing is the planning of a becoming background for entertaining. The room should always be gay and charming in color, but the color should be selected with due consideration of its becomingness to the host or hostess. Everyone has a right to look their best in their own dining room.

I do not favor the dark, heavy treatments and elaborate stuff hangings which seem to represent the taste of most of the men who go in for decorating nowadays. Nine times out of ten the dining room seems to be the gloomiest room in the house. I think it should be a place where the family may meet in gaiety of spirit for a pause in the vexatious happenings of the day. I think light tones, gay wallpapers, flowers and sunshine are of more importance than storied tapestries and heavily-carved furniture. These things are all very well for the house that has a small dining room and a gala dining room for formal occasions as well, but there are few such houses.

We New Yorkers have been so accustomed to the gloomy basement dining rooms of the conventional brownstone houses of the late eighties we forgot how nice a dining room can be. Even though the city dining room is now more fortunately placed in the rear of the second floor, it is usually overshadowed by other houses, and can be lightened only by skillful use of color in curtains, china, and so forth. Therefore, I think this is the one room in the city house where one can afford to use a boldly decorative paper. I like very much the Chinese rice papers with their broad sketchy decorations of birds and flowers. These papers are never tiresomely realistic and are always done in very soft colors or in soft shades of one color, and while if you analyze them they are very fantastic, the general effect is as restful as it is cheerful. You know you can be most cheerful when you are most rested!

The quaint landscape papers which are seen in so many New England dining rooms seem to belong with American Colonial furniture and white woodwork, prim silver and gold banded china. These landscape papers are usually gay in effect and make for cheer. There are many new designs less complicated than the old ones. Then, too, there are charming foliage papers, made up of leaves and branches and birds, which are very good.

While we may find color and cheer in these gay papers for gloomy city dining rooms, if we have plenty of light we may get more distinguished results with paneled walls. A large dining room may be paneled with dark wood, with a painted fresco, or tapestry frieze, and a ceiling with carved or painted beams, or perhaps one of those interesting cream-white ceilings with plaster beams judiciously adorned with ornament in low relief. Given a large dining room and a little money, you can do anything: you can make a room that will compare favorably with the traditional rooms on which we build. You have a right to make your dining room as fine as you please, so long as you give it its measure of light and air. But one thing you must have: simplicity! It may be the simplicity of a marble floor and tapestried walls and a painted ceiling, it may be the simplicity of white paint and muslin and fine furniture, but simplicity it must have. The furniture that is required in a dining room declares itself: a table and chairs. You can bring side tables and china closets into it, or you can build in cupboards and consoles to take their place, but there is little chance for other variation, and so the beginning is a declaration of order and simplicity.

The easiest way to destroy this simplicity is to litter the room with displays of silver and glass, to dot the walls with indifferent pictures. If you are courageous enough to let your walls take care of themselves and to put away your silver and china and glass, the room will be as dignified as you could wish. Remember that simplicity depends on balance and space. If the walls balance one another in light and shadow, if the furniture is placed formally, if walls and furniture are free from mistaken ornament, the room will be serene and beautiful. In most other rooms we avoid the "pairing" of things, but here pairs and sets of things are most desirable. Two console tables are more impressive than one. There is great decorative value in a pair of mirrors, a pair of candlesticks, a pair of porcelain jars, two cupboards flanking a chimney piece. You would not be guilty of a pair of wall fountains, or of two wall clocks, just as you would not have two copies of the same portrait in a room. But when things "pair" logically, pair them! They will furnish a backbone of precision to the room.

The dining room in the Iselin house is a fine example of stately simplicity. It is extremely formal, and yet there is about it none of the gloominess one associates with New York dining rooms. The severely paneled walls, the fine chimney piece with an old master inset and framed by a Grinling Gibbons carving, the absence of the usual mantel shelf, the plain dining table and the fine old lion chairs all go to make up a Georgian room of great distinction.

The person who cannot afford such expensive simplicity might model a dining room on this same plan and accomplish a beautiful room at reasonable expense. Paneled walls are always possible; if you can't afford wood paneling, paint the plastered wall white or cream and break it into panels by using a narrow molding of wood. You can get an effect of great dignity by the use of molding at a few cents a foot. A large panel would take the place of the Grinling Gibbons carving, and a mirror might be inset above the fireplace instead of the portrait. The dining table and chairs might give place to good reproductions of Chippendale, and the marble console to a carpenter-made one painted to match the woodwork.

The subject of proper furniture for a dining room is usually settled by the house mistress before her wedding bouquet has faded, so I shall only touch on the out-of-ordinary things here. Everyone knows that a table and a certain number of chairs and a sideboard of some kind "go together." The trouble is that everyone knows these things too well, and dining room conventions are so binding that we miss many pleasant departures from the usual.

My own dining room in New York is anything but usual, and yet there is nothing undignified about it. The room was practically square, so that it had a certain orderly quality to begin with. The rooms of the house are all rather small, and so to gain the greatest possible space I have the door openings at the extreme end of the wall, leaving as large a wall space as possible. You enter this room, then, through a door at the extreme left of the south wall of the room. Another door at the extreme right of the same wall leads to a private passage. The space left between the doors is thereby conserved, and is broken into a large central panel flanked by two narrow panels. The space above the doors is also paneled. This wall is broken by a console placed under the central panel. Above it one of the Mennoyer originals, which you may remember in the Washington Irving dining room, is set in the wall, framed with a narrow molding of gray. The walls and woodwork of the room are of exactly the same tone of gray—darker than a silver gray and lighter than pewter. Everything—color, balance, proportion, objects of art—has been uniformly considered.

Continuing, the east wall is broken in the center by the fireplace, with a mantel of white and gray marble. A large mirror, surmounted with a bas-relief in black and white, fills the space between mantel shelf and cornice. This mirror and bas-relief are framed with the narrow carved molding painted gray. Here again there is the beauty of balance: two Italian candlesticks of carved and gilded wood flank a marble bust on the mantel shelf. There is nothing more. On the right of the mirror, in a narrow panel, there is a wall clock of carved and gilded wood which also takes its place as a part of the wall, and keeps it.

The north wall is broken by two mirrors and a door leading into the service pantry. A large, fourfold screen, made of an uncut tapestry, shuts off the door. We need all the light the windows give, so there are no curtains except the orange-colored taffeta valances at the top. I devised sliding doors of mirrors that are pulled out of the wall at night to fill the recessed space of the windows. Ventilation is afforded by the open fireplace, and by mechanical means. You see, we do not occupy this house in the summer, so the mirrored windows are quite feasible.

The fourth wall has no openings, and it is broken into three large paneled spaces. A console has the place of honor opposite the fireplace, and above it there is a mirror like that over the mantel. In the two side panels are the two large Mennoyers. There are five of these in the room, the smaller ones flanking the chimney piece. You see that the salvation of this room depends on this careful repetition and variation of similar objects.

Color is brought into the room in the blue and yellow of the Chinese rug, in the chairs, and in the painted table. The chairs are painted a creamy yellow, pointed with blue, and upholstered with blue and yellow striped velvet. I do not like high-backed chairs in a dining room. Their one claim to use is that they make a becoming background, but this does not compensate for the difficulties of the service when they are used. An awkward servant pouring soup down one's back is not an aid to digestion, or to the peace of mind engendered by a good dinner.

The painted table is very unusual. The legs and the carved underframe are painted cream and pointed with blue, like the chairs, but the top is as gay as an old-fashioned garden, with stiff little medallions, and urns spilling over with flowers, and conventional blossoms picked out all over it. The colors used are very soft, blue and cream being predominant. The table is covered with a sheet of plate glass. This table is, of course, too elaborate for a simple dining room, but the idea could be adapted and varied to suit many color and furniture schemes.

Painted furniture is a delight in a small dining room. In the Colony Club I planned a very small room for little dinners that is well worth reproducing in a small house. This little room was very hard to manage because there were no windows! There were two tiny little openings high on the wall at one end of the room, but it would take imagination to call them windows. The room was on the top floor, and the real light came from a skylight. You can imagine the difficulty of making such a little box interesting. However, there was one thing that warmed my heart to the little room: a tiny ante-room between the hall proper and the room proper. The little ante-room I paneled in yellowish tan and gray. I introduced a sofa covered with an old brocade just the color of dried rose leaves—ashes of roses, the French call it—and the little ante-room became a fitting introduction to the dining room within.

The walls of the rooms were paneled in a delicious color between yellow and tan, the wall proper and the moldings being this color, and the panels themselves filled with a gray paper painted in pinky yellows and browns. These panels were done by hand by a man who found his inspiration in the painted panels of an old French ballroom. As the walls were unbroken by windows there was ample space for such decoration. A carpet of rose color was chosen, and the skylight was curtained with shirred silk of the same rose. The table was covered with rose-colored brocade, and over this, cobwebby lace, and over this, plate glass. There are two consoles in the room, with small cabinets above which hold certain *objets d'art* in keeping with the room.

Under the two tiny windows were those terrible snags we decorators always strike, the radiators. Wrongly placed, they are capable of spoiling any room. I concealed these radiators by building two small cabinets with panels of iron framework gilded to suggest a graceful metal lattice, and lined them with rose-colored silk. I borrowed this idea from a fascinating cabinet in an old French palace, and the result is worth the deception. The cabinets are nice in themselves, and they do not interfere with the radiation of the heat.

I have seen many charming country houses and farmhouses in France with dining rooms furnished with painted furniture. Somehow they make the average American dining room seem very commonplace and tiresome. For instance, I had the pleasure of furnishing a little country house in France and we planned the dining room in blue and white. The furniture was of the simplest, painted white, with a dark blue line for decoration. The corner cupboard was a little more elaborate, with a gracefully curved top and a large glass door made up of little panes set in a quaint design. There were several drawers and a lower cupboard. The drawers and the lower doors invited decorations a little more elaborate than the blue lines of the furniture, so we painted on gay little medallions in soft tones of blue, from the palest gray-blue to a very dark blue. The chair cushions were blue, and the china was blue sprigged. Three little pitchers of dark-blue luster were on the wall cupboard shelf and a mirror in a faded gold frame gave the necessary variation of tone.

A very charming treatment for either a country or small city dining room is to have corner cupboards of this kind cutting off two corners. They are convenient and unusual and pretty as well. They can be painted in white with a colored line defining the panels and can be made highly decorative if the panels are painted with a classic or a Chinese design. The decoration, however, should be kept in variations of the same tone as the stripe on the panels. For instance, if the stripe is gray, then the design should be in dark and light gray and blue tones. The chairs can be white, in a room of this kind, with small gray and blue medallions and either blue and white, or plain blue, cushions.

Another dining room of the same sort was planned for a small country house on Long Island. Here the woodwork was a deep cream, the walls the same tone, and the ceiling a little lighter. We found six of those prim Duxbury chairs, with flaring spindle backs, and painted them a soft yellow-green. The table was a plain one, with straight legs. We painted it cream and decorated the top with a conventional border of green adapted from the design of the china—a thick creamy Danish ware ornamented with queer little wavy lines and figures. I should have mentioned the china first, because the whole room grew from that. The rug was a square of velvet of a darker green. The curtains were soft cream-colored net. One wall was made up of windows, another of doors and cupboard, and against the other two walls we built two long, narrow consoles that were so simple anyone could accomplish them: simply two wide shelves resting on good brackets, with mirrors above. The one splendid thing in the room was a curtain of soft green damask that was pulled at night to cover the group of windows. Everything else in the room was bought for a song.

I have said much of cupboards and consoles because I think they are so much better than the awkward, heavy "china closets" and "buffets" and sideboards that dominate most dining rooms. The time has come when we should begin to do fine things in the way of building fitment furniture, that is, furniture that is actually or apparently part of the shell of the room. It would be so much better to build a house slowly, planning the furniture as part of the architectural detail. With each succeeding year the house would become more and more a part of the owner, illustrating their life. Of course, this would mean that the person who planned the developing of the house must have a certain architectural training, must know about scale and proportion, and something of general construction. Certainly charming things are to be created in this way, things that will last, things immeasurably preferable to the cheap jerry-built furniture which so soon becomes shabby, which has to be so constantly renewed. People accept new ideas with great difficulty, and my only hope is that they may grow to accept the idea of fitment furniture through finding the idea a product of their own; a personal discovery that comes from their own needs.

I have constantly recommended the use of our native American woods for panelings and wall furniture, because we have both the beautiful woods of our new world and tried and proven furniture of the old world, and what couldn't we achieve with such material available? Why do people think of a built-in cupboard as being less important than a detached piece of furniture? Isn't it a braggart pose, a desire to show the number of things you can buy? Of course it is a very foolish pose, but it is a popular one, this display of objects that are earmarked "expensive."

It is very easy to build cupboards on each side of a fireplace, for instance, making the wall flush with the chimney breast. This is always good architectural form. One side could have a desk which opens beneath the glass doors, and the other could have cupboards, both presenting exactly the same appearance when closed. Fitted corner cupboards, triangular or rounded, are also excellent in certain dining rooms.

Wall tables, or consoles, may be of the same wood as the woodwork or of marble, or of some dark polished wood. There are no more useful pieces of furniture than consoles, and yet we only see them in great houses. Why? Because they are simple, and we haven't yet learned to demand the simple. I have had many interesting old console tables of wrought iron support and marble tops copied, and I have designed others that were mere semicircles of white painted wood supported by four slender legs, but whether they be marble or pine the effect is always simple. There are charming consoles that have come to us from the eighteenth century, consoles made in pairs, so that they may stand against the wall as serving-tables, or be placed together to form one round table. This is a very good arrangement where people have one large living room or hall in which they dine and which also serves all the purpose of daily intercourse. This entirely removes any suggestion of a dining room, as the consoles may be separated and stand against the wall during the day.

Many modern houses are being built without the conventional dining room we have known so long, there being instead an open-air breakfast room which may be glazed in winter and screened in summer. People have come to their senses at last, and realize that there is nothing so pleasant as eating outdoors. The annual migration of Americans to Europe is responsible for the introduction of this excellent custom. French houses are always equipped with some outdoor place for eating. Some of them have, in addition to the enclosed porch, a fascinating pavilion built in the garden, where breakfast and tea may be served. Modern mechanical conveniences and the inexpensive electric apparatus make it possible to serve meals at this distance from the house and keep them hot in the meantime. One may prepare one's own coffee and toast at table, with the green trees and flowers and birds all around.

Eating outdoors makes for good health and long life and good temper, everyone knows that. The simplest meal seems a gala affair when everyone is radiant and cheerful, whereas a long and elaborate meal served indoors is usually depressing.

XIV.
THE BEDROOM

In olden times people rarely slept in their bedrooms, which were mostly *chambres de parade*, where everyone was received and much business was transacted. The real bedroom was usually a smallish closet nearby. These *chambres de parade* were very splendid, the beds raised on a dias, and hung with fine damasks and tapestries—tapestries thick with bullion fringes. The horror of fresh air felt by our ancestors was well-illustrated here. No draughts from ill-constructed windows or badly-hung doors could reach the sleeper in such a bed.

This was certainly different from our modern ideas of hygiene: in those days furniture that could not be hastily moved was of little importance. The bed was usually a mere frame of wood, made to be covered with valuable hangings which could easily be packed and carried away on occasions that too often arose in the troublesome days of the early Middle Ages. The benches and tables one sees in many foreign palaces today are covered with gorgeous lengths of velvet and brocade. This is a survival of the custom when furniture was merely so much baggage. With the early eighteenth century, however, there came into being *les petits apartments*, in which the larger space formerly accorded the bedroom was divided into ante-chamber, salon or sitting room, and the bedroom. Very often the bed was placed in an alcove, and the heavy brocades and bullion embroideries were replaced by linen or cotton hangings.

When Oberkampf established himself at Jouy in 1760 France took first place in the production of these printed linens and cottons. This was the beginning of the age of chintz and of the delightful decorative fabrics that are so suited to our modern ideas of hygiene. It seems to me there are no more charming stuffs for bedroom hangings than these simple fabrics, with their enchantingly fanciful designs. Think of the changes one could have with several sets of curtains to be changed at will, as Marie Antoinette used to do at the Petit Trianon. How amusing it would be in our own modern houses to change the bed coverings, window curtains, and so forth, twice and three times a year! I like these loose slipcovers and curtains better than the usual hard upholstery, because if properly planned the slips can be washed without losing their color or their lines.

Charming eighteenth-century prints that are full of valuable hints as to furniture and decorations for bedrooms can be found at most French shops. The series known as "Moreau le Jeun" is full of suggestion. Some of the interiors shown are very grand, it is true, but many are simple enough to serve as models for modern apartments. A set of these pictures will do much to give one an insight into the decoration of the eighteenth century, a vivid insight that can be obtained in no other way, perhaps.

I do not like the very large bedrooms, dear to the plans of the American architect. I much prefer the space divided. I remember once arriving at the Ritz Hotel in London and being given temporarily a very grand royal suite, overlooking the park, until the smaller quarters I had reserved should be ready for me. How delighted I was at first with all the huge vastness of my bedroom! My appreciation waned, however, after a despairing morning toilet spent in taking many steps back and forth from dressing table to bathroom, and from bathroom to hang-closets, and I was glad indeed, when, at the end of several hours, I was comfortably housed in my smaller and humbler quarters.

I think the ideal bedroom should be planned so that a small ante-chamber should separate it from the large outside corridor. The ideal arrangement is an ante-chamber opening on the boudoir, or sitting room, then the bedroom, with its dressing room and bath in back. This outer chamber insures quiet and privacy, no matter how small it may be. It may serve as a clothes-closet, by filling the wall with cupboards, and concealing them with mirrored doors. The ante-chamber need not be a luxury, if you plan your house carefully. It is simply a little well of silence and privacy between you and the hall outside.

To go on with my ideal bedroom: the walls, I think, should be simply paneled in wood, painted gray or cream or white, but if wood cannot be afforded, a plastered wall, painted or distempered in some soft tone, is the best solution. You will find plain walls and gay chintz hangings very much more satisfying than walls covered with flowered papers and plain hangings, for the simple reason that a design repeated hundreds of times on a wall surface becomes very, very tiresome, but the same design in a fabric is softened and broken by the folds of the material, and you will never get the annoying sense of being impelled to count the figures.

A bedroom with an Elizabethan paper does not belong to the "busy" class, for while the design is decorative in the extreme you are not aware of an emphatic repeat. This is really an old chintz design, and is very charming in blues and greens and grays on a cream ground. I have seen bedrooms papered with huge scrolls and seashells, many times enlarged, that suggest the noisy and methodical thumping of a drum. I cannot imagine anyone sleeping calmly in such a room!

This bedroom is eminently suited to the needs of a man. The hangings are of a plain, soft stuff, accenting one of the deep tones of the wall covering, and the sash curtains are of white muslin. The furniture is of oak, of the Jacobean period. The bed is true to its inspiration, with turned legs and runners, and slatted head and foot boards. The legs and runners of the bed were really inspired by the chairs and tables of the period. This is an excellent example of the modern furniture that may be adapted from old models. It goes without saying that the beds of that period were huge, cumbersome affairs, and this adapted bed is really more suitable to modern needs in size and weight and line than the original one.

There are so many inspirations for bedrooms nowadays that one finds it most difficult to decide on any one scheme. One of my greatest joys in planning the Colony Club was that I had opportunity to furnish so many bedrooms. And they were small, pleasant rooms, too, not the usual impersonal boxes that are usually planned for club houses and hotels. I worked out the plan of each bedroom as if I were to live in it myself, and while they all differed in decorative schemes the essentials were the same in each room: a comfortable bed, with a small table beside it to hold a reading light, a clock, and a telephone; a *chaise-longue* for resting; a long mirror somewhere; a dressing table with proper lights and a glass-covered top; a writing table, carefully equipped, and the necessary chairs and stools. Some of the bedrooms had no connecting baths, and these were given wash stands with bowls and pitchers of clear glass. Most of these bedrooms were fitted with mahogany four-post beds, pie crust tables, colonial highboys, gay chintzes and such, but there were several rooms of entirely different scheme.

Perhaps most fascinating of them all is the bird room. The walls are covered with an Oriental paper patterned with marvelous blue-and-green birds, birds of paradise and parakeets perched on flowering branches. The black lacquer furniture was especially designed for the room. The rug and the hangings are of jade green. I wonder how this seems to read of—I can only say it is a very gay and happy room to live in!

There is another bedroom in pink and white, which would be an adorable room for a young girl. The bed is of my own design, a simple white painted metal bed. There is a *chaise-longue*, upholstered in the pink-and-white-striped chintz of the room. The same chintz is used for window hangings, bedspread, and so forth. There is a little spindle-legged table of mahogany, and another table at the head of the bed which contains the reading light. There is also a little white stool, with a cushion of the chintz, beside the bed. The dressing-table is so simple that anyone might copy it—it is a chintz-hung box with a sheet of plate glass on top, and a white framed mirror hung above it. The electric lights in this room are cleverly made into candlesticks, which are painted to match the chintz. The writing table is white, with a mahogany chair in front of it.

Another bedroom has a narrow four-post bed of mahogany, with hangings of China blue sprigged with small pink roses. There was another in green and white. In every case these bedrooms were equipped with rugs of neutral and harmonious tone. The dressing tables were always painted to harmonize with the chintzes or the furniture. Wherever possible there was an open fireplace. Roomy clothes closets added much to the comfort of the room, and there was always a couch of delicious softness, or a *chaise-longue*, and lounging chairs which invited repose.

Nothing so nice has happened in a long time as the revival of painted furniture, and the application of quaint designs to modern beds and chairs and chests. You may find inspiration in a length of chintz, in an old fan, in a faded print—anywhere! The main thing is to work out a color plan for the background—the walls, the furniture, and the rugs—and then you can draw or stencil the chosen designs wherever they seem to belong, and paint them in with dull tones and soft colors, rose and buff and blue and green and a little bit of gray and cream and black. Or, if you aren't even as clever as that (and you probably are!) you can decorate your painted furniture with narrow lines of color: dark green on a light green ground; dark blue on yellow; any color on gray or cream—there are infinite possibilities of color combinations. In some of the rooms the posy garlands on the chest of drawers were inspired by a lamp jar. This furniture was carefully planned, as may be seen by the little urns on the bedposts, quite in the manner of the Brothers Adam, but delightful results may be obtained by using any simple modern cottage furniture and applying fanciful decorations.

Be wary of hanging many pictures in your bedroom. I give this advice cheerfully, because I know you will hang them anyway (I do) but I warn you you will spoil your room if you aren't very stern with yourself. Somehow the pictures we most love, small prints and photographs and things, look spotty on our walls. We must group them to get a pleasant effect. Keep the framed photographs on the writing table, the dressing table, the mantel, etc., but do not hang them on the walls. If you have small prints that you feel you must have, hang them flat on the wall, well within the line of vision. They should be low enough to be examined, because usually such pictures are not decorative in effect, but exquisite in detail. The fewer pictures the better, and in the guest room fewer still!

I planned a guest room for the top floor of a New York house that is very successful. The room was built around a pair of appliques made from two old Chinese sprays of metal flowers. I had small electric light bulbs fitted among the flowers, mounted them on carved wood brackets on each side of a good mantel mirror and worked out the rest of the room from them. The walls were painted bluish-green, the woodwork white. Just below the molding at the top of the room there was a narrow border (four inches wide) of a mosaic-like pattern in blue and green. The carpet rug is of a blue-green tone. The hangings are of an alluring Chinoiserie chintz, and there are several Chinese color prints framed and hanging in the narrow panels between the front windows. The furniture is painted a deep cream pointed with blue and green, and the bed covering is of a pale turquoise taffeta.

Another guest room was done in gentian blue and white, with a little buff and rose-color in small things. This room was planned for the guests of the daughter of the house, so the furnishings were naïvely and adorably feminine. The dressing table was made of a long, low box, with a glass top and a valance so crisp and flouncing that it suggested a young lady in crinoline. The valance was of chintz in gentian blue and white. The white mirror frame was decorated with little blue lines and tendrils. Surely any girl would grow pretty with dressing before such an enchanting affair! And simple—why, she could hinge the mirrors together, and make the chintz ruffle, and enamel shelves white, and do every bit of it except cut the plate glass. Of course the glass is very clean and nice, but an enameled surface with a white linen cover would be very pleasant.

The same blue-and-white chintz was used for the hangings and bed coverings. Everything else in the room was white except the thick cream rug with its border of blue and rose and buff, and the candlesticks and appliques which repeated those colors.

There is a chintz I love to use called the Green Feather chintz. It is most decorative in design and color, and such an aristocratic sort of chintz you can use it on handsome old sofas and four-post beds that would scorn a more commonplace chintz. Mrs. Payne Whitney has a most enchanting bed covered with the Green Feather chintz, one of those great beds that depend entirely on their hangings for effect, for not a bit of the wooden frame shows. Mrs. Frederick Havemeyer has a similar bed covered with a Chinoiserie chintz. These great beds are very beautiful in large rooms, but they would be out of place in small ones. There are draped beds, however, that may be used in smaller rooms. In a bedroom in the Crocker house in Burlingame, California, where I used a small draped bed with charming effect. This bed is placed flat against the wall, like a sofa, and the drapery is adapted from that of a Louis XVI room. The bed is of gray painted wood, and the hangings are of blue and cream chintz lined with blue taffetas. I used the same idea in a rose and blue bedroom in a New York house. In this case, however, the bed was painted cream white and the large panels of the head and foot boards were filled with a rose and blue chintz. The bedspread was of deep rose-colored taffetas, and from a small canopy above the bed four curtains of the rose and blue chintz, lined with the taffetas, are pulled to the four corners of the bed. This novel arrangement of draperies is very satisfactory in a small room.

In my own house the bedrooms open into dressing rooms, so much of the usual furniture is not necessary. My own bedroom, for instance, is built around the same old Breton bed I had in the Washington Irving House. The bed dominates the room, but there are also a *chaise-longue*, several small tables, many comfortable chairs, and a real fireplace. The business of dressing takes place in the dressing room, so there is no dressing table there, but there are long mirrors filling the wall spaces between windows and doors. Miss Marbury's bedroom is just over mine, and is a sunshiny place of much rose and blue and cream. Her rooms are always full of blue, just as my rooms are always full of rose color. This bedroom has cream woodwork and walls of a bluish-gray, cream painted furniture covered with a mellow sort of rose-and-cream chintz, and a Persian rug made up of blue and cream. The curtains at the windows are of plain blue linen bordered with a narrow blue and white fringe. The lighting fixtures are of carved wood, pointed in polychrome. The most beautiful thing in the room is a fifteenth-century painting, the Madonna of Bartolomeo Montagna, which has the place of honor over the mantel.

I haven't said a word about our nice American Colonial bedrooms, because all of you know their beauties and requirements as well as I. The great drawback to the stately old furniture of our ancestors is the space it occupies. Haven't you seen a fine old four-post bed simply overflowing a little room? Fortunately, the furniture makers are designing simple beds of similar lines, but lighter build, and these beds are very lovely. The owner of a massive old four-post bed is justly proud of it, but our new beds are built for a new service and a new conception of hygiene, and so must find new lines and curves that will be friendly to the old dressing tables and highboys and chests of drawers.

When we are fortunate enough to inherit great old houses, of course we will give them proper furniture—if we can find it.

I remember a house in New Orleans that had a full dozen spacious bedrooms, square, closetless chambers that opened into small dressing rooms. One of them, I remember was absolutely bare of wall and floor, with a great Napoleon bed set squarely in the center of it. There was the inevitable mosquito net canopy, here somehow endowed with an unexpected dignity. One felt the room had been made for sleeping, and nothing but sleeping, and while the bed was placed in the middle of the floor to get all the air possible, its placing was a master stroke of decoration in that great white-walled room. It was as impressive as a royal bed on a dias.

We are getting more sensible about our bedrooms. There is no doubt about it. For the last ten years there has been a dreadful epidemic of brass beds, a mistaken vogue that came as a reaction from the heavy walnut beds of the last generation. White painted metal beds came first, and will last always, but they weren't good enough for people of ostentatious tastes, and so the vulgar brass bed came to pass. Why we should suffer brass beds in our rooms, I don't know! The plea is that they are more sanitary than wooden ones. Hospitals must consider sanitation first, last, and always, and they use white iron beds. And why shouldn't white iron beds, which are modest and unassuming in appearance, serve for homes as well? The truth is that the glitter of brass appeals to the untrained eye. But that is passing. Go into the better shops and you will see! Recently there was a spasmodic outbreak of silver-plated beds, but I think there won't be a vogue for this newest object of bad taste. It is a little too much!

If your house is clean and you intend to keep it so, a wooden bed that has some relation to the rest of your furniture is the best bed possible. Otherwise, a white painted metal one. There is never an excuse for a brass one. Indeed, I think the three most glaring errors we Americans make are rocking chairs, lace curtains, and brass beds.[1]

XIV. THE BEDROOM

XV.
THE DRESSING ROOM AND THE BATH

DRESSING ROOMS AND CLOSETS should be necessities, not luxuries, but alas! our architects' ideas of the importance of large bedrooms have made it almost impossible to incorporate the proper closets and dressing places people really require.

In the foregoing chapter on bedrooms I advised the division of a large bedroom into several smaller rooms: ante-chamber, sitting room, sleeping room, dressing room and bath. The necessary closets may be built along the walls of all these little rooms, or if there is sufficient space, one long, airy closet may serve for all one's personal belongings. Of course, such a suite of rooms is possible only in large houses. But even in simple houses a small dressing room can be built into the corner of an average-sized room.

In France every woman dresses in her *cabinet de toilette*; it is one of the most important rooms in the house. No self-respecting French woman would dream of dressing in her sleeping room. The little *cabinet de toilette* need not be much larger than a closet, if the closets are built ceiling high, and the doors are utilized for mirrors. Such an arrangement makes for great comfort and privacy. Here I find that most of my countrywomen dress in their bedrooms. I infinitely prefer the separate dressing room, which means a change of air, and which can be thoroughly ventilated. If one sleeps with the bedroom windows wide open, it is a pleasure to have a warm dressing room to step into.

I think the first thing to be considered about a dressing room is its utility. Here no particular scheme of decoration or over-elaboration of color is in place. Everything should be very simple, very clean and very hygienic. The floors should not be of wood, but may be of marble or mosaic cement or clean white tiles, with a possible touch of color. If the dressing room is bathroom also, there should be as large a bath as is compatible with the size of the room. The combination of dressing room and bathroom is successful only in those large houses where each bedroom has its bath. I have seen such rooms in modern American houses that were quite as large as bedrooms, with the supreme luxury of open fireplaces. Think of the comfort of having one's bath and of making one's toilet before an open fire! This is an outgrowth of our passion for bedrooms that are so be-windowed they become sleeping porches, and we may leave their chill air for the comfortable warmth of luxurious dressing rooms.

If I were giving advice as to the furnishing of a dressing room, in as few words as possible, I should say: "Put in lots of mirrors, and then more mirrors, and then more!" Indeed, I do not think one can have too many mirrors in a dressing room. Long mirrors can be set in doors and wall panels, so that one may see one's self from hat to boots. Hinged mirrors are lovely for sunny wall spaces, and for the tops of dressing tables. I have made so many of them. One of green and gold lacquer was made to be used on a plain green enameled dressing table placed squarely in the recesses of a great window. I also use small mirrors of graceful contour to light up the dark corners of dressing rooms.

Have your mirrors so arranged that you get a good strong light by day, and have plenty of electric lights all around the dressing mirrors for night use. In other words, know the worst before you go out! In my own dressing room the lights are arranged just as I used to have them long ago in my theater dressing room when I was on the stage. I can see myself back, front and sides before I go out. Really, it is a comfort to be on friendly terms with your own back hair! I lay great stress on the mirrors and plenty of lights, and yet more lights. Oh, the joy, the blessing of electric light! I think everyone would like to dress always by a blaze of electric light, and be seen only in the soft luminosity of candlelight—how lovely we would all look, to be sure! It is a great thing to know the worst before one goes out, so that even the terrors of the arc lights before our theaters will be powerless to dismay us.

If there is room in the dressing room, there should be a sofa with a slipcover of some washable fabric that can be taken off when necessary. This sofa may be the simplest wooden frame, with a soft pad, or it may be a *chaise-longue* of elegant lines. The *chaise-longue* is suitable for bedroom or dressing room, but it is an especially luxurious lounging place when you are having your hair done.

A man came to me just before Christmas, and said, "Do tell me something to give my wife. I cannot think of a thing in the world she hasn't already." I asked, "Is she a lady of habits?" "What!" he said, astonished. "Does she enjoy being comfortable?" I asked. "Well, rather!" he smiled. And so I suggested a *couvre-pieds* for her *chaise-longue*. Now I am telling you of the *couvre-pieds* because I know all women love exquisite things, and surely nothing could be more delicious than my *couvre-pieds*. Literally, it is a "cover for the feet," a sort of glorified and diminutive coverlet, made of the palest of pink silk, lined with the soft long-haired white fur known as mountain tibet, and interlined with down. The coverlet is bordered with a puffing of French lace, and the top of it is encrusted with little flowers made of tiny French picot ribbons, and quillings of the narrowest of lace. It is supposed to be thrown over your feet, fur side down, when you are resting or having your hair done.

You may devise a little coverlet for your own sofa, whether it be in your bedroom, your boudoir, or your dressing room, that will be quite as useful as this delectable *couvre-pieds.* I saw some amusing ones recently, made of gay Austrian silks, lined with astonishing colors and bound with puffings and flutings of ribbon of still other colors. A coverlet of this kind would be as good as a trip away from home for the woman who is bored and wearied. No matter how drab and commonplace her house might be, she could devise a gay quilt of one of the enchanting new stuffs and wrap herself in it for a holiday hour. One of the most amusing ones was of turquoise blue silk, with stiff flowers of violet and sulfur yellow silk, and the binding was a puffing of violet ribbons. The color fairly made me gasp, at first, but then it became fascinating, and finally irresistible. I sighed as I thought of the dreary patchwork quilts of our great-grandmothers. How they would have marveled at our audacious use of color, our frank joy in it!

Of course the most important thing in the dressing room is the dressing table. I place my dressing table against a group of windows, not near them, whenever it is possible. I have used plate glass tops on many of them, and mirrors for tops on others, for you can't have too many mirrors or too strong a light for dressing. We must see ourselves as other will see us.

My own dressing table contains many drawers, one of which is fitted with an inkwell, a tray for pens and pencils, and a sliding shelf on which I write. This obviates going into another room to answer hurried notes when one is dressing. Beside the dressing table stands the tall hat-stand for the hat I may be wearing that day.

When the maid prepares the dress that is to be worn, she puts the hat that goes with the toilette on the tall single stand. Another idea is the little hollow table on casters that can easily be slipped under the dressing table, where it is out of the way. All the little ugly things that make one lovely can be kept in this table, which can have a lid if desired, and even a lock and key. I frequently make them with a glass bottom, as they do not get stained or soiled, and can be washed.

There are lots of little dodges that spell comfort for the dressing room of the person who wants comfort and can have luxury. There is the hot-water towel rack, which is connected with the hot-water system of the house and which heats the towels, and incidentally the dressing room. This is a boon if you like a hot bath sheet after a cold plunge on a winter's morning. Another modern luxury is a wall cabinet fitted with glass shelves for one's bottles and sponges and powders. There seems to be no end to the little luxuries that are devised for the person who makes a proper toilet. Who can blame them for loving the business of making themselves attractive, when everyone offers encouragement?

A closet is absolutely necessary in the dressing room, and if space is precious every inch of its interior may be fitted with shelves and drawers and hooks, so that no space is wasted. The outside of the closet door may be fitted with a mirror, and narrow shelves just deep enough to hold one's bottles, may be fitted on the inside of the door. If the closet is very shallow, the inner shelves should be hollowed out to admit the bottle shelves when the door is closed. Otherwise the bottles will be smashed the first time the door is slammed carelessly. This bottle closet has been one of my great successes in small apartments, where bathroom and dressing room are one, and where much must be accomplished in a small space.

In the more modern apartments the tub is placed in a recess in the wall of the bathroom, leaving more space for dressing purposes. This sort of combination dressing room should have waterproof floor and wall, and no fripperies. There should be a screen large enough to conceal the tub, and a folding chair that may be placed in the small closet when it is not in use.

When the bathroom is too small to admit a dressing table and chair and the bedroom is quite large, a good plan is the building of a tiny room in the one corner of the window. Of course this little dressing box must have a window. I have used this plan many times with excellent results. Another scheme, when the problem was entirely different, and the dressing room was too large for comfort, was to line three walls of it with closets, the fourth wall being filled with windows. These closets were narrow, each having a mirrored panel in its door. This is the ideal arrangement, for there is ample room for all one's gowns, shoes, hats, veils, gloves, etc., each article having its own specially-planned shelf or receptacle. The closets are painted in gay colors inside, and the shelves are fitted with thin perfumed pads. They are often further decorated with bright lines of color, which is always amusing to whomever opens a door. Hat stands and bags are covered with the same chintzes employed in the dressing room proper. Certain of the closets are fitted with the English tray shelves, and each tray has its sachet. The hangers for gowns are covered in the chintz or brocade used on the hat stands. This makes an effective ensemble whether brocades or printed cottons are used, if the arrangement is orderly and full of gay color.

One of the most successful gown closets I have done is a long narrow closet with a door at each end, really a passageway between a bedroom and a boudoir. Long poles run the length of the closet, with curtains that enclose a passage from door to door. Back of these curtains are long poles that may be raised or lowered by pulleys. Each gown is placed on its padded hanger, covered with its muslin bag, and hung on the pole. The pole is then drawn up so that the tails of the gowns will not touch the dust of the floor. This is a most orderly arrangement for the woman of many gowns.

The straightaway bathroom that one finds in apartments and small houses is difficult to make beautiful, but may be made airy and clean-looking, which is more important. I had to make such a bathroom a little more attractive recently, and it was a very pleasant job. I covered the walls with a waterproof stuff of white, figured with a small black polka dot. The woodwork and the ceiling were painted white. All around the door and window frames I used a two-inch border of ivy leaves, also of waterproof paper, and although I usually abominate borders I loved this one. A plain white-framed mirror was also painted with green ivy leaves, and a glass shelf above the wash bowl was fitted with glass bottles and dishes with labels and lines of clear green. White muslin curtains were hung at the window, and a small white stool was given a cushion covered with green and white ivy-patterned chintz. The floor was painted white, and a solid green rug was used. The towels were cross-stitched with the name of the owner in the same bright green. The room, when finished, was cool and refreshing, and had cost very little in money, and not so very much in time and labor.

I think that in country houses where there is not a bathroom with each bedroom there should be a very good washstand provided for each guest. When a house party is in progress, for instance, and everyone comes in from tennis or golf or what not, eager for a bath and fresh clothes, washstands are most convenient. Why shouldn't a washstand be just as attractively furnished as a dressing table? Just because they have been so ugly we condemn them to eternal ugliness, but it is quite possible to make the washstand interesting to look upon as well as serviceable. It isn't necessary to buy a "set" of dreadful crockery. You can assemble the necessary things as carefully as you would assemble the outfit for your writing table. Go to the pottery shops, the glass shops, the silversmiths, and you will find dozens of bowls and pitchers and small things. A clear glass bowl and pitcher and the necessary glasses and bottles can be purchased at any department store. The French peasants make an apple-green pottery that is delightful for a washstand set. So many of the china shops have large shallow bowls that were made for salad and punch, and pitchers that were made for the dining table, but there is no reason why they shouldn't be used on the washstand. I know one wash basin that began as a Russian brass pan of flaring rim. With it is used an old water can of hammered brass, and brass dishes glass-lined, to hold soaps and sponges. It is only necessary to desire the unusual thing, and you'll get it, though much searching may intervene between the idea and its achievement.

The washstand itself is not such a problem. A pair of dressing tables may be bought, and one fitted up as a washstand, and the other left to its usual use.

In the Colony Club there are a number of bathrooms, but there are also washstands in those rooms that have no private bath. Each bathroom has its fittings planned to harmonize with the connecting bedroom, and the clear glass bottles are all marked in the color prevailing in the bedroom. Each bathroom has a full-length mirror, and all the conveniences of a bathroom in a private house. In addition to these rooms there is a long hall filled with small *cabinets de toilette* which some clever woman dubbed "prinkeries." These are small rooms fitted with dressing tables, where out-of-town members may freshen their toilets for an occasion. These little prinkeries would be excellent in large country houses, where there are so many motoring guests who come for a few hours only, dust-laden and travel-stained, only to find that all the bedrooms and dressing rooms in the house are being used by the family and the house guests.

A description of the pool of the Colony Club is hardly within the province of this chapter, but so many amazing Americans are building themselves great houses incorporating theaters and Roman baths, so many people are building club houses, so many others are building palatial houses that are known as private schools, perhaps the swimming pool will soon be a part of all large houses. This pool occupies the greater part of the basement floor of the Club house, the rest of the floor being given over to little rooms where one may have a shampoo or massage or a dancing lesson or what not before or after one's swim. The pool is twenty-two by sixty feet, sunken below the level of the marble floor. The depth is graded from four feet to deep water, so that good and bad swimmers may enjoy it. The marble margin of floor surrounding the pool is bordered with marble benches, placed between the white columns. The walls of the great room are paneled with mirrors, so that there are endless reflections of columned corridors and pools and shimmering lights. The ceiling is covered with a light trellis hung with vines, from which hang great greenish-white bunches of grapes holding electric lights. One gets the impression of myriads of white columns, and of lights and shadows infinitely far-reaching. Surely the old Romans knew no pleasanter place then this city-enclosed pool.

XVI.
THE SMALL APARTMENT

THIS IS THE AGE of the apartment. Not only in the great cities, but in the smaller centers of civilization the apartment has come to stay. Modern people demand simplified living, and the apartment reduces the mechanical business of living to its lowest terms. A decade ago the apartment was considered a sorry makeshift in America, though it has been successful abroad for more years than you would believe. We Americans have been accustomed to so much space about us that it seemed a curtailment of family dignity to give up our gardens, our piazzas and halls, our cellars and attics, our front and rear entrances. Now we are wiser. We have just so much time, so much money and so much strength, and it behooves us to make the best of it. Why should we give our time and strength and enthusiasm to drudgery, when our housework were better and more economically done by machinery and cooperation? Why should we stultify our minds with doing the same things thousands of times over, when we might help ourselves and our friends to happiness by intelligent occupations and amusements? The apartment is the solution of the living problems of the city, and it has been a direct influence on the houses of the towns, so simplifying the small town business of living as well.

Of course, many of us who live in apartments either have a little house or a big one in the country for the summer months, or we plan for one some day! So hard does habit die—we cannot entirely divorce our ideas of home from gardens and trees and green grass. But I honestly think there is a reward for living in a slice of a house: people who have lived long in the country sometimes take the beauty of it for granted, but those who have been hedged in by city walls get the fine joy of out-of-doors when they are out of doors, and a pot of geraniums means more than a whole garden to a person who has been denied the privilege of watching things grow.

The modern apartment is an amazing illustration of the rapid development of an idea. The larger ones are quite as magnificent as any houses could be. I have recently furnished a Chicago apartment that included large and small salons, a huge conservatory, and a great group of superb rooms that are worthy of a palace. There are apartment houses in New York that offer suites of fifteen to twenty rooms, with from five to ten baths, at yearly rentals that approximate wealth to the average man, but these apartments are for the few, and there are hundreds of thousands of apartments for the many that have the same essential conveniences.

One of the most notable achievements of the apartment house architects is the duplex apartment, the little house within a house, with its two-story high living room, its mezzanine gallery with service rooms ranged below and sleeping rooms above, its fine height and spaciousness. Most of the duplex apartments are still rather expensive, but some of them are to be had at rents that are comparatively low—rents are always comparative, you know.

Fortunately, although it is a far cry financially from the duplex apartment to the tidy three-room flat of the model tenements, the "modern improvements" are very much the same. The model tenement offers compact domestic machinery, and cleanliness, and sanitary comforts at a few dollars a week that are not to be had at any price in many of the fine old houses of Europe. The peasant who has lived on the plane of the animals with no thought of cleanliness, or indeed of anything but food and drink and shelter, comes over here and enjoys improvements that our stately ancestors of a few generations ago would have believed magical. Enjoys them—they do say he puts his coal in the bath tub, but his grandchildren will be different, perhaps!

But enough of apartments in general. This chapter is concerned with the small apartment sought by young people who are just beginning housekeeping. You want to find just the proper apartment, of course, and then you want to decorate and furnish it. Let me beg of you to demand only the actual essentials: a decent neighborhood, good light and air, and at least one reasonably large room. Don't demand perfection, for you won't find it. Make up your mind just what will make for your happiness and comfort, and demand that. You can make any place livable by furnishing it wisely. And, oh, let me beg of you, don't buy your furniture until you have found and engaged your apartment! It is bad enough to buy furniture for a house you haven't seen, but an apartment is a place of limitations, and you can so easily mar the place by buying things that will not fit in. An apartment is so dependent upon proper fittings, skillfully placed, that you may ruin your chances of a real home if you go ahead blindly.

Before you sign your lease, be sure that the neighborhood is not too noisy. Be sure that you will have plenty of light and air and heat. You can interview other tenants, and find out about many things you haven't time or the experience to anticipate. Be sure that your landlord is a reasonable human being who will consent to certain changes, if necessary, who will be willing for you to build in certain things, who will cooperate with you in improving the property, if you go about it tactfully.

Be sure that the woodwork is plain and unpretentious, that the lighting fixtures are logically placed, and of simple construction. (Is there anything more dreadful than those colored glass domes, with fringes of beads, that landlords so proudly hang over the imaginary dining table?) Be sure that the plumbing is in good condition, and beware the bedroom on an air shaft—better pay a little more rent and save the doctor's bills. Beware of false mantels, and grotesque grille-work, and imitation stained glass, and grained woodwork. You couldn't be happy in a place that was false to begin with.

Having found just the combination of rooms that suggest a real home to you, go slowly about your decorating.

It is almost imperative that the woodwork and walls should have the same finish throughout the apartment, unless you wish to find yourself living in a crazy-quilt of unfriendly colors. I have seen four-room apartments in which every room had a different wallpaper and different woodwork. The "parlor" was papered with poisonous-looking green paper, with imitation mahogany woodwork; the dining room had walls covered with red burlap and near-oak woodwork; the bedroom was done in pink satin finished paper and bird's-eye maple woodwork, and the kitchen was bilious as to woodwork, with bleak gray walls. Could anything be more mistaken?

You can make the most commonplace rooms livable if you will paint all your woodwork cream, or gray, or sage green, and cover your walls with a paper of very much the same tone. Real hardwood trim isn't used in ordinary apartments, so why not do away with the badly-grained imitation and paint it? You can look through thousands of samples of wallpapers, and you will finally have to admit that there is nothing better for everyday living than a deep cream, a misty gray, a tan or buff paper.

You may have a certain license in the papering of your bedrooms, of course, but the living rooms—hall, dining room, living room, drawing room, and so forth—should be pulled together with walls of one color. In no other way can you achieve an effect of spaciousness—and spaciousness is the thing of all other things most desirable in the crowded city. You must have a place where you can breathe and fling your arms about!

When you have it really ready for furnishing, get the essentials first; do with a bed and a chest of drawers and a table and a few chairs, and add things gradually, as the rooms call for them.

Make the best of the opportunities offered for built-in furniture before you buy another thing. If you have a built-in china closet in your dining room, you can plan a graceful built-in console table to serve as a buffet or serving table, and you will require only a good table—not too heavily built—and a few chairs for this room. There is rarely a room that would not be improved by built-in shelves and inset mirrors.

Of course, I do not advise you to spend a lot of money on someone else's property, but why not look the matter squarely in the face? This is to be your home. You will find a number of things that annoy you—life in any city furnishes annoyances. But if you have one or two reasonably large rooms, plenty of light and air, and respectable surroundings, make up your mind that you will not move every year. That you will make a home of this place, and then go ahead and treat it as a home! If a certain recess in the wall suggests bookshelves, don't grudge the few dollars necessary to have the bookshelves built in! You can probably have them built so that they can be removed, on that far day when this apartment is no longer your home, and if you have a dreadful wallpaper don't hide behind the silly plea that the landlord will not change it. Go without a new hat, if necessary, and pay for the paper yourself.

Few apartments have fireplaces, and if you are fortunate enough to find one with a real fireplace and a simple mantel shelf you will be far on the way toward making a home of your group of rooms. Of course your apartment is heated by steam, or hot air, or something, but an open fire of coal or wood will be very pleasant on chilly days, and more important still your home will have a point of departure—the hearth.

If the mantel shelf is surmounted by one of those dreadful monstrosities made up of gingerbread woodwork and distressing bits of mirrors, convince your landlord that it will not be injured in the removing, and store it during your residence there. Have the space above the mantel papered like the rest of the walls, and hang one good picture, or a good mirror, or some such thing above your mantel shelf, and you will have offered up your homage to the Spirit of the Hearth.

When you do begin to buy furniture, buy compactly, buy carefully. Remember that you will not require the furniture your mother had in a sixteen-room house. You will have no hall or piazza furnishings to buy, for instance, and therefore you may put a little more into your living room things. The living room is the nucleus of the modern apartment. Sometimes it is studio, living room and dining room in one. Sometimes living room, library and guest room, by the grace of a comfortable sleeping couch and a certain amount of drawer or closet space. At any rate, it will be more surely a living room than a similar room in a large house, and therefore everything in it should count for something. Do not admit an unnecessary rug, or chair, or picture, lest you lose the spaciousness, the dignity of the room. An overstuffed chair will fill a room more obviously than a grand piano—if the piano is properly, and the chair improperly placed.

I think it unwise to try to work out a cut-and-dried color plan in a small apartment. If your floors and walls are neutral in tone, you can introduce dozens of soft colors into your rooms.

Don't buy massive furniture for your apartment! Remember that a few good chairs of willow will be less expensive and more decorative than the heavy, stuff chairs usually chosen by inexperienced people. Indeed, I think one big armchair, preferably of the wing variety, is the only big chair you will require in the living room. A fireside chair is like a grandfather's clock; it gives so much dignity to a room that it is worth a dozen inferior things. Suppose you have a wing chair covered with dull-toned corduroy, or linen, or chintz; a large willow chair with a basket pocket for magazines or your sewing things; a stool or so of wood, with rush or cane seats; and a straight chair or so—perhaps a painted Windsor chair, or a rush-bottomed mahogany chair, or a low-back chair of brown oak—depending on the main furniture of the room, of course. You won't need anything more, unless you have space for a comfortable couch.

If you have mahogany things, you will require a little mahogany table at the head of the couch to hold a reading lamp—a sewing table would be excellent. A pie crust or turn top table for tea, or possibly a "nest" of three small mahogany tables. A writing table or book table built on very simple lines will be needed also. If you happen to have a conventional writing desk, a gate-leg table would be charming for books and things.

The wing chair and willow chairs, and the hourglass Chinese chairs, will go beautifully with mahogany things or with oak things. If most of your furniture is to be oak, be sure and select well-made pieces stained a soft brown and waxed. Oak furniture is delightful when it isn't too heavy. A large gate-leg table of dark brown oak is one of the most beautiful tables in the world. With it you would need a bench of oak, with cane or rush seat; a small octagonal, or butterfly oak table for your couch end, and one or two Windsor chairs. Oak demands simple, wholesome surroundings, just as mahogany permits a certain feminine elegance. Oak furniture invites printed linens and books and brass and copper and pewter and gay china. While mahogany may be successfully used with such things, it may also be used with brocade and fragile china and carved chairs.

Use chintzes in your apartment, if you wish, but do not risk the light ones in living rooms. A chintz or printed linen of some good design on a ground of mauve, blue, gray or black will decorate your apartment adequately, if you make straight side curtains of it, and cover one chair and possibly a stool with it. Don't carry it too far. If your rooms are small, have your side curtains of coarse linen or raw silk in dull blue, orange, brown, or whatever color you choose as the key color of your room, and then select a dark chintz with your chosen color dominant in its design, and cover your one big chair with that.

The apartment hall is most difficult, usually long and narrow and uninteresting. Don't try to have furniture in a hall of this kind. A small table near the front door, a good tile for umbrellas, etc., a good mirror—that is all. Perhaps a place for coats and hats, but some halls are too narrow for a card table.

The apartment with a dining room entirely separated from the living room is very unusual, therefore I am hoping that you will apply all that I have said about the treatment of your living room to your dining room as well. People who live in apartments are very foolish if they cut off a room so little used as a dining room and furnish it as if it belonged to a huge house. Why not make it a dining room and book room, using the big table for reading, between meals, and having your bookshelves so built that they will be in harmony with your china shelves? Keep all your glass and silver and china in the kitchen, or butler's pantry, and display only the excellent things—the old china, the pewter tankard, the brass caddy, and so forth—in the dining room.

However, if you have a real dining room in your apartment, do try to have chairs that will be comfortable, for you can't afford to have uncomfortable things in so small a space! Windsor chairs and rush-bottom chairs are best of all for a simple dining room, I think, though the revival of painted furniture has brought about a new interest in the old flare-back chairs, painted with dull, soft-colored posies on a ground of dull green or gray or black. These chairs would be charming in a small cottage dining room, but they might not "wear well" in a city apartment.

If your apartment has two bedrooms, why not use one of them for two single beds, with a night stand between, and the other for a dressing room? Apartment bedrooms are usually small, but charming furniture may be bought for small rooms. Single beds of mahogany with slender posts; beds of painted wood with inset panels of cane; white iron beds, wooden beds painted with quaint designs on a ground of some soft color—all these are excellent for small rooms. It goes without saying that a small bedroom should have plain walls, papered or painted in some soft color. Flowered papers, no matter how delightful they may be, make a small room seem smaller. Self-toned striped papers and the "gingham" papers are sometimes very good. The nicest thing about such modest walls is that you can use gay chintz with them successfully.

Use your bedrooms as sleeping and dressing rooms, and nothing more. Do not keep your sewing things there—instead, a big sewing basket will add to the homelike quality of your living room. Keep the bedroom floor bare, except for a bedside rug, and possibly one or two other rugs.

This, of course, does not apply to the large bedroom, I am prescribing for the usual small one. Place your bed against the side wall, so that the morning light will not be directly in your eyes. A folding screen covered with chintz or linen will prove a godsend.

Perhaps you will have a guest room, but I doubt it. Most people find it more satisfactory and less expensive to send their guests to a nearby hotel than to keep an extra room for a guest. The guest room is impractical in a small apartment, but you can arrange to take care of an overnight guest by planning your living room wisely.

As for the kitchen—that is another story. It is impossible to go into that subject. And anyway, you will find the essentials supplied for you by the landlord. You won't need my advice when you need a broom or a coffee pot or a saucepan—you'll go buy it![1]

XVII.
REPRODUCTIONS OF ANTIQUE FURNITURE AND OBJECTS OF ART

ONE MUST HAVE PRESERVED many naïve illusions if one may believe in all the "antiques" that are offered in the marketplaces of the world today. Even the greatest connoisseurs are caught napping sometimes, as in the case of the famous crown supposedly dating to the fifth century, B.C., which was for a brief period one of the treasures of the Louvre. Its origin was finally discovered, and great was the outcry! It had been traced to a Viennese artisan, a worker in the arts and crafts.

Surely, if the great people in the Louvre could be so deceived it is obvious that the amateur collector has little chance at the hands of the dealers in old furniture and other objects of art. Fortunately, the greatest dealers are quite honest. They tell you frankly if the old chair you covet is really old, if it has been partially restored, or if it is a copy, and they charge you accordingly. At these dealers a small table of the Louis XVI period, or a single chair covered in the original tapestry, may cost as much as a man in modest circumstances would spend on his whole house. Almost everything outside these princely shops (salons is a better word) is false, or atrociously restored. Please remember I am not referring to reputable dealers, but to the smaller fry, whose name is legion, in whose shops the unwary seeker after bargains is sure to be taken in.

Italy is, I think, the greatest workshop of fraudulent reproductions. It has an output that all Europe and America can never exhaust. Little children on the streets of Naples still find simpletons of ardent faith who will buy scraps of old plaster and bits of paving stones that are alleged to have been excavated in Pompeii.

In writing about antiques it is not easy to be consistent, and any general conclusion is impossible. Certain reproductions are objectionable, and yet they are certainly better than poor originals, after all. The simplest advice is the best and easiest to follow: The less a copy suggests an attempt at "artistic reproduction," the more literal and mechanical it is in its copy of the original, the better it is. A good photograph of a fine old painting is superior to the average copy in oils or watercolors. A chair honestly copied from a worm-eaten original is better for domestic purpose than the original. The original, the moment its usefulness is past, belongs in a museum. A plaster cast of a great bust is better than the same object copied in marble or bronze by an average sculptor. And so it goes. Think it out for yourself.

It may be argued that the budding collector is as happy with a false object and a fake bauble as if they possessed the real thing, and therefore it were better to leave them to their illusions; that it is their own fault; that it is so much the worse for them if they are deceived. But—you can't leave the innocent lamb to the slaughter, if you can give it a helping hand. If they must be a collector, let them be first a collector of the many excellent books now published on old furniture, china, rugs, pewter, silver, prints, the things that will come their way. You can't begin collecting one thing without developing an enthusiasm for the contemporary things. Let them study the museum collections, visit the private collections, consult recognized experts. If they are serious, they will gradually acquire the intuition of knowing the genuine from the false, the worthwhile from the worthless, and once they have that knowledge, instinct, call it what you will, they can never be satisfied with imitations.

The collection and association of antiques and reproductions should be determined by the collector's sense of fitness, it seems to me. Everyone should depend on whatever instinct for rightness, for suitability, they may possess. If they find that they dare not risk their individual opinion, then let them be content with the things they *know* to be both beautiful and useful, and leave the subtler decisions for someone else. For instance, there are certain objects that are obviously the better for age, the objects that are softened and refined by a bloom that comes from usage.

An old rug has a softness that a new one cannot imitate. An old copper kettle has an uneven quality that has come from years of use. A new kettle may be quite as useful, but age has given the old one a certain quality that hanging and pounding cannot reproduce. A pewter platter that has been used for generations is dulled and softened to a glow that a new platter cannot rival.

What charm is to a person, the vague thing called quality is to an object of art. We feel it, though we may not be able to explain it. An old Etruscan jar may be reproduced in form, but it would be silly to attempt the reproduction of the crudenesses that gave the old jar its real beauty. In short, objects, that depend on form and fine workmanship for their beauty may be successfully reproduced, but objects that depend on imperfections of workmanship, on the crudeness of primitive fabrics, on the fading of vegetable dyes, on the bloom that age alone can give, should not be imitated. We may introduce a reproduction of a fine bust into our rooms, but an imitation of a Persian tile or a Venetian vase is absurd on the face of it.

The antiques the average American householder is interested in are the old mahogany, oak, and walnut things that stand for the oldest period of our own particular history. It is only the wealthy collector who goes abroad and buys masses of old European furniture, real or sham, who is concerned with the merits and demerits of French and Italian furniture.

The native problem is the so-called Colonial mahogany that is always alleged to be Chippendale or Heppelwhite, or Sheraton, regardless! There must be thousands of these alleged antiques in New York shops alone!

It goes without saying that only a very small part of it can be really old. As for it having been made by the men whose names it bears, that is something no reputable dealer would affirm. The Chippendales, father, son and grandson, published books of designs which were used by all the furniture makers of their day.

No one can swear to a piece of furniture having been made in the workshops of the Chippendales. Even the pieces in the Metropolitan Museum are marked "Chippendale Style" or "In the Sheraton manner," or some such way. If the furniture is in the style of these makers, and if it is really old, you will pay a small fortune for it. But even then you cannot hope to get more than you pay for, and you would be very silly to pay for a name! After all, Chippendale is a sort of god among amateur collectors of American furniture, but among more seasoned collectors he is not by any means placed first. He adapted and borrowed and produced some wonderful things, but he also produced some monstrosities, as you will see if you visit the English museums.

Why then lend yourself to possible deception? Why pay for names when museums are unable to buy them? If your object is to furnish your home suitably, what need have you of antiques?

The serious amateur will fight shy of miracles. If they admire the beauty of line of a fine old Heppelwhite bed or Sheraton sideboard, they will have reproductions made by an expert cabinetmaker. The new piece will not have the soft darkness of the old, but the owner will be planning that soft darkness for their grandchildren, and in the meantime they will have a beautiful thing to live with. The age of a piece of furniture is of great value to a museum, but for domestic purposes, use and beauty will do. How fine your home will be if all the things within it have those qualities!

Look through the photographs shown on these pages: there are many old chairs and tables, but there are more new ones. I am not one of these decorators who insist on originals. I believe good reproductions are more valuable than feeble originals, unless you are buying your furniture as a speculation. You can buy a reproduction of a Chippendale ladder-back chair for about twenty-five dollars, but an original chair would cost at least a hundred and fifty, and then it would be "in the style and period of Chippendale." It might amuse you to ask the curator of one of the British museums the price of one of the Chippendales by Chippendale. It would buy you a tidy little acreage. Stuart and Cromwellian chairs are being more and more reproduced. These chairs are made of oak, the Stuart ones with seats and backs of cane, the Cromwellian ones with seats and backs of tapestry, needlework, corded velvet, or some such handsome fabric. These reproductions may be had at from twenty-five to seventy-five dollars each. Of course, the cost of the Cromwellian chairs might be greatly increased by expensive coverings.

There is a graceful Louis xv sofa in the Petit Trianon that I have copied many times. The copy is as beautiful as the original, because this sort of furniture depends upon exquisite design and perfect workmanship for its beauty. It is possible that a modern craftsman might not have achieved so graceful a design, but the perfection of his workmanship cannot be gain-said. The frame of the sofa must be carved and then painted and gilded many times before it is ready for the brocade covering, and the cost of three hundred dollars for the finished sofa is not too much. The original could not be purchased at any price.

Then there is the Chinese lacquer furniture of the Chippendale period that we are using so much now. The process of lacquering is as tedious today as it ever was, and the reproductions sell for goodly sums. A tall secretary of black and gold lacquer may cost six hundred dollars. You can imagine what an eighteenth-century piece would cost!

The person who said that a taste for old furniture and bibelots was "worse than a passion, it was a vice," was certainly near the truth! It is an absorbing pursuit, an obsession, and it grows with what it feeds on. As in objects of art, so in old furniture, the supply will always equal the demand of the unwary. The serious amateurs will fight shy of all miracles and content themselves with excellent reproductions. Nothing later than the furniture of the eighteenth century is included in the term "old furniture." There are many fine cabinetmakers in the early nineteenth century, but from them until the last decade the horrors that were perpetrated have never been equaled in the history of household decorations.

I fancy the furniture of the mid-Victorian era will never be coveted by collectors, unless someone should build a museum for the freakish objects of house furnishing. America could contribute much to such a collection, for surely the black walnut era of the nineteenth century will never be surpassed in ugliness and bad taste, unless—rare fortune—there should be a sudden epidemic of appreciation among cabinetmakers, which would result in their taking the beautiful wood in the black walnut beds and wardrobes and such and making it over into worthwhile things. It would be a fine thing to release the mistreated, velvety wood from its grotesqueries, and give it a renaissance in graceful cabinets, small tables, foot-stools, and the many small things that could be so easily made from huge unwieldy wardrobes and beds and *bureaux*.

The workers of today have their eyes opened. They have no excuse for producing unworthy things, when the greatest private collections are loaned or given outright to the museums. The new wing of the Metropolitan Museum in New York houses several fine old collections of furniture, the Hoentschel collection, for which the wing was really planned, having been given to the people of New York by Mr. Pierpont Morgan. This collection is an education in the French decorative arts. Then, too, there is the Bolles collection of American furniture presented to the museum by Mrs. Russell Sage.

I have no quarrel with honest dealers who are making fine and sincere copies of such furniture, and selling them as copies. There is no deception here, we must respect these people as we respect the workers of the eighteenth century: we give them respect for their masterly workmanship, their appreciation of the best things, and their fidelity to the masterpieces they reproduce.

Not so long ago the New York papers published the experience of a gentleman who bought a very beautiful divan in a European furniture shop. He paid for it—you may be sure of that!—and he could hardly wait for its arrival to show it to his less fortunate neighbors. Within a few months something happened to the lining of the divan, and he discovered on the inside of the frame the maker's name and address. Imagine his chagrin when he found that the divan had been made at a furniture factory in his own country. You can't be sorry for him, you feel that it served him right.

This is an excellent example of the vain collector who cannot judge for himself, but will not admit it. He has not developed his sense of beauty, his instinct for excellence of workmanship. He thinks that because he has the money to pay for the treasure, the treasure must be genuine—hasn't he chosen it?

I can quite understand the pleasure that goes with furnishing a really old house with objects of the period in which the house was built. A New England farmhouse, for instance, may be an inspiration to the owner, and you can understand the quest of old-fashioned rush-bottomed chairs and painted settles and quaint mirrors and blue homespun coverlets. You can understand the man who falls heir to a good, square old Colonial house who wishes to keep his furnishings true to the period, but you cannot understand the crying need for eighteenth-century furniture in a modern shingle house, or the desire for old spinning wheels and battered kitchen utensils in a Spanish stucco house, or Chippendale furniture in a forest bungalow.

I wish people generally would study the oak and walnut furniture of old England, and use more reproductions of these honest, solid pieces of furniture in their houses. Its beauty is that it is "at home" in simple American houses, and yet by virtue of its very usefulness and sturdiness it is not out of place in a room where beautiful objects of other periods are used. The long oak table that is so comfortably ample for books and magazines and flowers in your living room may be copied from an old refectory table—but what of it? It fulfills its new mission just as frankly as the original table served the monks who used it.

The soft brown of oak is a pleasure after the over-polished mahogany of a thousand rooms. I do not wish to condemn Colonial mahogany furniture, you understand. I simply wish to remind you that there are other woods and models available. French furniture of the best type represents the supreme art of the cabinetmaker, and is incomparable for formal rooms, but I am afraid the time will never come when French furniture will be interchangeable with the oak and mahogany of England and America.

In short, the whole thing should be a matter of taste and suitability. If you have a few fine old things that have come to you from your ancestors—a grandfather's clock, an old portrait or two—you are quite justified in bringing good reproductions of similar things into your home. The effect is the thing you are after, isn't it? Then, too, you will escape the awful fever that makes any antique seem desirable, and in buying reproductions you can select really comfortable furniture. You will be independent of the dreadful vases and candelabra and steel engravings "of the period," and will feel free to use modern prints and Chinese porcelains and willow chairs and anything that fits into your home. I can think of no slavery more deadly to one's sense of humor than collecting antiques indiscriminately![1]

XVIII.
THE ART OF TRELLIAGE

When I planned the trellis room of the Colony Club in New York I had hard work finding workmen who could appreciate the importance of crossing and re-crossing little strips of green wood, of arranging them to form a mural decoration architectural in treatment. This trellis room was, I believe, the first in America to be so considered, though the use of trellis is as old as architecture in Japan, China, Arabia, Egypt, Italy, France and Spain.

The earliest examples of trellis work shown are in certain Roman frescoes. In Pompeii the mural paintings give us a very good idea of what some of the Roman gardens were like. In the entrance hall of the house of Sallust is represented a garden with trellised niches and bubbling fountains. Representations that have come down to us in documents show that China and Japan both employed the trellis in their decorative schemes. You will find a most daring example on your old blue willow plate, if you will look closely enough. The bridge over which the flying princess goes to her lover is a good model, and could be built in many gardens. Even a tiny modern garden, yours or mine, might hold this fairy bridge.

Almost all Arabian decorations have their basis in trellis design or arabesques filled in with the intricate tracery that covers all their buildings. If we examine the details of the most famous of the old Moorish buildings that remain to us, the mosque at Cordova and the Alhambra at Granada, we shall find them full of endless trellis suggestions. Indeed, there are many documents still extant showing how admirably trellis decoration lends itself to the decoration of gardens and interiors. There are dozens of examples of niches built to hold fine busts. Pavilions and summer houses, the quaint gazebos of old England, the graceful screens of trellis that terminate a long garden path, the arching gateways crowned with vines—all these may be reproduced quite easily in American gardens.

The first trellis work in France was inspired by Italy, but the French gave it a perfection of architectural character not found in other countries. The manuscript of the "Romance of the Rose," dating back to the fifteenth century, contains the finest possible example of trellis in a medieval garden. Most of the old French gardens that remain to us have important trellis construction. At Blois one still sees the remains of a fine trellis covering the walls of the kitchen gardens. Wonderful and elaborate trellis pavillons, each containing a statue, often formed the centers of very old gardens. These garden houses were called gazebos in England, and Temples d'Amour (Temples of Love) in France, and the statue most often seen was the god of Love. In the Trianon gardens at Versailles there is a charming Temple d'Amour standing on a tiny island, with four small canals leading to it.

A knowledge of the history of trelliage and an appreciation of its practical application to modern needs is a conjurer's wand—you can wave it and create all sorts of ephemeral constructions that will last your time a pleasure. You may give your trellis any poetic shape your vision may take. You may dream and realize enchanting gardens, with clipped hedges and trellis walls. You may transform a commonplace porch into a gay garden room, with a few screens of trellis and many flower boxes of shrubs and vines. Here indeed is a delightful medium for your fancy!

Trelliage and lattice work are often used as interchangeable items, but mistakenly, for any carpenter who has the gift of precision can build a good lattice, but a trellis must have architectural character. Trellis work is not necessarily flimsy construction; the light chestnut laths that were used by the old Frenchmen and still remain to us prove that.

Always in a garden I think one must feel one has not come to the end, one must go on and on in search of new beauties and the hidden delights we feel sure must be behind the clipped hedges or the trellis walls. Even when we come to the end we are not quite sure it is the end, and we steep ourselves in seclusion and quiet, knowing full well that tomorrow or tonight perhaps when the moon is up and we come back as we promise ourselves to do, surely we shall see that ideal corner that is the last word of the perfection of our dream garden—that delectable spot for which we forever seek!

We can bring back much of the charm of the old-time gardens by a judicious use of trellis. It is suitable for every form of outdoor construction. A new garden can be subdivided and made livable in a few months with trellis screens, where hedges, even of the quick-growing privet, would take years to grow. The entrance to the famous maze at Versailles, now, alas, utterly destroyed, was in trellis, and I have reproduced in our own garden at Villa Trianon, in Versailles, the entrance arch and doors, all in trellis. Our high garden fence with its curing gate is also in trellis, and you can imagine the joy with which we watched the vines grow, climbing over the gatetop as gracefully as if they too felt the charm of the curving tracery of green strips, and cheerfully added the decoration of their leaves and tendrils.

Our outdoor trellis is at the end of the Villa Trianon garden, in line with the terrace where we take our meals. This trellis was rebuilt many times before it satisfied me, but now it is my greatest joy. The niches are planned to hold two old statues and several prim box trees. I used very much the same constructive design on one of the walls of the Colony Club trellis room, but there a fountain has the place of honor. Formal pedestals surmounted by gracefully curved urns, box trees, statues, marble benches, fountains—all these belong to the formal outdoor trellis.

The trellis is primarily suitable for garden architecture, but it may be fitted to interior uses most skillfully. Pictures of the trellis room in the Colony Club have been shown so often it is not necessary to repeat more than one of them. The room is long and high, with a floor of large red tiles. The walls and ceiling are covered with rough gray plaster, on which the green strips of wood are laid. The wall space is entirely covered with the trellis design broken into ovals, which hold lighting fixtures—grapes and leaves in cloudy glass and green enamel. The long room leads up to the ivy-covered trellis of the fountain wall, a perfect background for the fountain, a bowl on the brim of which is poised a youthful figure, upheld by two dolphins. The water spills over into a little pool, banked with evergreens. Ivy has been planted in long boxes along the wall, and climbs to the ceiling, where the plaster is left bare, save for the trellised cornice and the central trellis medallion, from which is suspended an enchanting lantern made up of green wires and ivy leaves and little white flames of electric light.

The roof garden of the Colony Club is latticed in a simple design we all know. This is lattice, not trellis, and in no way should be confounded with the trellis room on the entrance floor. This white-painted lattice covers the wall space. Growing vines are placed along the walls and clamber to the beams. The glass ceiling is supported by white beams. There are always blossoming flowers and singing birds in this room. The effect is spring-like and joyous on the bleakest winter day. The room is heated by two huge stoves of green Majolica brought over from Germany when other heating systems failed. Much of the furniture is covered with a grape-patterned chintz and a green-and-white-striped linen. The ceiling lights are hidden in huge bunches of pale green grapes.

I recently planned a most beautiful trellis room for a New York City house. The room is long and narrow, with walls divided into panels by upright classic columns. The lower wall space between the column is covered with a simple green lattice, and the upper part is filled with little mirrors framed in narrow green moldings, arranged in a conventional design which follows the line of the trellis. One end of the room is made up of two narrow panels of the trellis with a fireplace between. On the opposite wall the middle panel is a background for a delightful wall fountain. The fretwork of mirrors which takes the place of frieze in the room is continued all around the four walls. One of the walls is filled entirely with French doors of plate glass, beneath the mirrored frieze; the other long wall has the broad, central panel cut into two doors of plate glass, and stone benches placed against the two trellised panels flanking the doors. The ceiling is divided into three great panels of trellis, and from each of the three panels a lantern is suspended.

In the Guinness house in New York there is a little hallway wainscoted in white with a green trellis covering the wall space above. Against this simple trellis—it really is a lattice—a number of plaster casts are hung. In one corner an old marble bowl holds a grapevine, which has been trained over the walls. The floor is of white tiles, with a narrow Greek border of black and white. This decoration of a little hall might be copied very easily.

The architects are building nowadays many houses that have a sun room, or conservatory, or breakfast room. The smallest cottage may have a little breakfast room done in green and white lattice, with green painted furniture and simple flower boxes. I have had furniture of the most satisfactory designs made for my trellis rooms. Green painted wood with cane insets seems most suitable for the small rooms, and the marbles of the old trellised Temples d'Amour may be replaced by cement benches in our modern trellis pavilions.

There is so much of modern furniture that is refreshing in line and color, and adapted to these sun rooms. There is a desk made by Aitchen, a notable furniture designer in London, which I have used in a sun room. The desk is painted white, and is decorated with heavy lines of dark green. The drawer front and the doors of the little cupboard are filled with cane. The knobs are of green. This desk would be nice in a white writing room in a summer cottage, though it was planned for a trellis room. It could be used as a dressing table, with a bench or chair of white, outlined in green, and a good mirror in white and green frame. Another desk I have made is called a jardiniere table, and was designed for Mrs. Ogden Armour's garden room at Lake Forest. The desk, or table, is painted gray, with faint green decorations. At each end of the long top there is a sunken zinc-lined box to hold growing plants. Between the flower boxes there is the usual arrangement of the desk outfit, blotter pad, paper rack, ink pots, and so forth. The spaces beneath the flower boxes are filled with shelves for books and magazines. This idea is thoroughly practicable for any garden room, and is so simple that it could be constructed by anyone who knows how to use tools.

I had the pleasure recently of planning a trellis room for Mrs. Ormond-Smith's house at Center Island, New York. Here indeed is a garden room with a proper environment. It is as beautiful as a room very well can be within, and its great arched windows frame vistas of trees and water which take their place as a part of the room, ever-changing landscapes that are always captivating. This trellis room is beautifully proportioned, and large enough to hold four long sofas and many chairs and tables of wicker and painted wood. The grouping of the sofas and the long tables made to fit between them is most interesting. These tables are extremely narrow and just the length of the sofas, and are built after the idea of Mrs. Amour's garden room desk, with flower boxes sunk in the ends. The backs of two sofas are placed against the long sides of the table, which holds a reading lamp and books in addition to its masses of flowers at the ends. Two such groups divide the room into three smaller rooms. Small tables and chairs are pulled up to the sofas, making conversation centers, or comfortable places for reading.

The trellis work covers the spaces between windows and doors, and follows the contour of the arches. The ceiling is bordered with the trellis, and from a great square of it in the center a lamp is suspended. The wall panels are broken by appliques that suggest the bounty of summer, flowers and leaves and vines in wrought and painted iron. There are pedestals surmounted by marbles against some of the panels, and a carved bracket supporting a magnificent bust high on one of the wider panels. The room is classic in its fine balance and its architectural formality, and modern in its luxurious comfort and its refreshing color. Surely there could be no pleasanter room for whiling away a summer day.[1]

XIX.
VILLA TRIANON

THE STORY OF the Villa Trianon is a fairy-tale come true. It came true because we believed in it—many fairy stories are ready and waiting to come true if only people will believe in them long enough.

For many years Elizabeth Marbury and I had spent our summers in that charming French town, Versailles, before we had any hope of realizing a home of our own there. We loved the place, with its glamour of romance and history, and we prowled around the old gardens and explored the old houses, and dreamed dreams and saw visions.

One old house that particularly interested us was the villa that had once been the home of the Duce de Nemours, son of Louis Philippe. It was situated directly on the famous Park of Versailles, which is, as everyone knows, one of the most beautiful parks in all the world. The villa had not been lived in since the occupancy of de Nemours. Before the villa came to de Nemours it had been a part of the royal property that was portioned out to Mesdames de France, the disagreeable daughters of Louis XV. You will remember how disagreeable they were to Marie Antoinette, and what a burden they made her life. I wish our house had belonged to a more romantic people; Madame du Barry or Madame de Pompadour would have suited me better!

How many, many times we peeped through the high iron railing at this enchanted domain, sleeping like the castle in the fairy tale. The garden was overgrown with weeds and shrubbery, the house was shabby and sadly in need of paint. We sighed and thought how happy would be our fortune if we might some day penetrate the mysteries of the tangled garden and the abandoned villa. Little did we dream that this would one day be our home.

We first went to Versailles as casual summer visitors and our stay was brief. We loved it so much that the next summer we went again, this time for the season, and found ourselves members of a happy pension family. Then we decided to rent an apartment of our own, for the next year, and soon we were considering the leases of houses, and finally we arrived at the supreme audacity of negotiating for the purchase of one. We had a great friend in Versailles, Victorien Sardou, the novelist and playwright so honored by the people of France. His wonderful house at Marly le Roi was a constant joy to us, and made us always more eager for a permanent home of our own in the neighborhood. Sardou was as eager for the finding of our house as we were, and it was he who finally made it possible for us to buy our historic villa. He did everything for us, introduced us to his friends, wonderful and brilliant people, gave us liberally of his charm and knowledge, and finally gave us the chance to buy this old house and its two acres of gardens.

The negotiations for the house were long and tedious. Our offer was an insult, a joke, a ridiculous affair to the man who had the selling of it! He laughed at us, and demanded twice the amount of our offer. We were firm, outwardly, and refused to meet him halfway, but secretly we spent hours and hours in the old house, sitting patiently on folding campstools, and planning the remaking of the house as happily as children playing make-believe.

I remember vividly the three of us, Miss Marbury, Sardou, and I, standing in the garden on a very rainy day. Sardou was bounding up and down, saying: "Buy it, buy it! If you don't buy it before twelve o'clock tomorrow I will buy it myself!" We were standing there soaking wet, perfectly oblivious to the downpour, wondering if we dared do such an audacious thing as to purchase property so far from our American anchorage.

Well, we bought it, and at our own price, practically, and for eight years we have been restoring the house and gardens to their seventeenth-century beauty. Sardou was our neighbor, and his wonderful château at Marly, overlooking the valley and terraces of St. Germain, was a never-failing surprise to us, so full was it of beauty and charm, so flavored with the personality of its owner. Sardou was of great help to us when we finally purchased our house. His fund of information never failed us, there seemed to be no question he could not answer. He was quite the most erudite man I have ever known. He had as much to say about the restoration of our house as we. He introduced us to Monsieur de Nolhac, the conservator of the Château de Versailles, who gave us the details of our villa as it had been a century and a half ago, and helped us remake the garden on the lines of the original one. He loaned us pictures and documents, and we felt we were living in a modern version of the *Sleeping Beauty*, with the sleeping villa for a heroine.

Our house had always been called "Villa Trianon," and so we kept the name, but it should not be confused with the Grand Trianon or the Petit Trianon. Of course everyone knows about the Park at Versailles, but everyone forgets, so I shall review the history of the Park briefly, that you may appreciate our thrills when we really owned a bit of it.

Louis XIV selected Versailles as the site for the royal palace when it was a swampy, uninteresting little farm. Louis XIII had built a château there in 1627, but had done little to beautify the flat acres surrounding it. Louis the Magnificent lavished fortunes on the laying-out of his new park. The Grand Trianon was built for Madame de Maintenon in 1685, and from this time on, for a full century, the Park of Versailles was the most famous royal residence in the world.

The Petit Trianon was built by Louis XV for Madame du Barry. Later, during the reign of Louis XVI, Marie Antoinette, who was then Queen, tiring of court etiquette and scorning the stately rooms of Versailles, persuaded her husband to make over to her the Petit Trianon. Here she built a number of little rustic cottages, where she and the ladies of her court, dressed in calicoes, played at being milkmaids. They had a little cottage called the "Laiterie," where white cows with their gilded horns were brought in to be milked. Here, too, little plays were presented in a tiny theater where only the members of the court were admitted. The Queen and her brother, Comte de Provence, were always the chief actors.

Our villa adjoins the Park proper. In our deeds to the two acres there is a clause which reserves a right-of-way for the King! The deed is worded like the old lease that dates back to 1750, and so one day we may have to give a King a right-of-way through our garden, if France becomes a monarchy again. Anyone who knows the French at all knows how dearly they cherish the dream of a monarchy.

One of the small houses we found on our small estate had once been a part of the *hameau* of Marie Antoinette. We have had this little house rebuilt and connected to the villa, and now use it as a guest house. It is very charming, with its walls covered with lattices and ivy.

Villa Trianon, like most French houses, is built directly on the street, leaving all the space possible for the garden. The façade of the villa is very simple, it reminds you of the square houses of the American Colonial period, except that there is no "front porch," as is inevitable with us in America. The entrance gate and the stone wall that surround the place give an interest that our detached and hastily-built American houses lack. The wall is really a continuation of the façade of the villa, and is surmounted by a black iron railing. Vines and flowers that have flourished and died and flourished again for over a century climb over the wall and through the graceful railing, and give our home an air of permanence that is very satisfying. After all, that is the secret of Europe's fascination for us Americans—the ever-present suggestion of permanence. We feel that houses and gardens were planned and built for centuries, not for the passing pleasure of one brief lifetime. We people them with ghosts that please us, and make histories for them that are always romantic and full of happiness. The survival of an old house and its garden through centuries of use and misuse is always an impressive and dramatic discovery to us: it gives us courage to add our little bit to the ultimate beauty and history, it gives us excuse to dream of the fortunate people who will follow us in other centuries, and who will, in turn, bless us for our part in the remaking of one old house and garden.

There was much to do! We hardly knew where to begin, the house was in such wretched condition. The roof was falling in, and the debris of years was piled high inside, but the walls and the floors were still very beautiful and as sound as ever, structurally. We had the roof restored, the debris removed, and the underbrush weeded out of the garden, and then we were ready to begin the real business of restoration.

The house is very simply planned. There is a broad hall that runs straight through it, with dining room and housekeepers' hall on the right, and four connecting salons on the left. These salons are charming rooms, with beautiful paneling and over-doors, and great arches framed in delicate carvings. First comes the writing room, then the library, then the large and small salons. The rooms opening on the back of the house have long

French windows that open directly upon the terrace, where we have most of our meals. The note of the interior of the house is blue, and there are masses of blue flowers in the garden. The interior woodwork is cream, pointed in blue, and there are blues innumerable in the rugs and curtains and *objets d'art*. There must be a hundred different shades of blue on this living floor, I think. We have tried to restore the rooms to a Louis XV scheme of decoration. The tables and cabinets are of the fine polished woods of the period. Some of the chairs are roomy affairs of carved and painted wooden frames and brocade coverings, but others are modern easy chairs covered in new linens of old designs, linens that were designed for just such interiors when Oberkampf first began his designing at Jouy. The mirrors and lighting fixtures are, of course, designed to harmonize with the carvings of the woodwork. Monsieur de Nolhac and Sardou were most helpful to us when such architectural problems had to be solved.

We have not used the extravagant lace curtains that seem to go with brocades and carvings, because we are modern enough not to believe in lace curtains. And we find that thin white muslin ones give our brocades and tapestries a chance to assert their decorative importance. Somehow, lace curtains give a room such a dressed-up-for-company air that they quite spoil the effect of beautiful fabrics. We have a few fine old Savonyerie carpets that are very much at home in this house, and so many interesting eighteenth-century prints we hardly know how to use them.

Our bedrooms are very simple, with their white panelings and chintz hangings. We have furnished them with graceful and feminine things, delicately carved mirror frames and inlaid tables, painted beds, and chests of drawers of rosewood or satinwood. We feel that the ghosts of the fair ladies who live in the Park would adore the bedrooms and rejoice in the strange magic of electric lights. If the ghosts should be confronted with the electric lights their surprise would not be greater than was the consternation of our builders when we demanded five bathrooms. They were astounded, and assured us it was not necessary, it was not possible. Indeed, it seemed that it was hardly legal to give one small French house five American bathrooms. We fought the matter out, and got them, however.

We determined to make the house seem a part of the garden, and so we built a broad terrace across the rear of the villa. You step directly from the long windows of the salon and dining room upon the terrace, and before you is spread out our little garden, and back of that, through an opening in the trees, a view of the Château, our never-failing source of inspiration.

The terrace is built of tiles on a cement foundation. Vines are trained over square column-like frames of wire, erected at regular intervals. Between the edge of the terrace and the smooth green lawn there is a mass of blue flowers. We have a number of willow chairs and old stone tables here, and you can appreciate the joy of having breakfast and tea on the terrace with the birds singing in the boughs of the trees.

I have written at length in the other chapters of my ideas of house furnishing, and in this one I want to give you my ideas of garden building. True, we had the old garden plan to work from, and trees two hundred years old, and old vine-covered walls. Who couldn't accomplish a perfect garden with such essentials, people said! Well, it wasn't so easy as it seems. You can select furnishings for a room with fair success, because you can see and feel textures, and colors, and the lines of the furniture and curtains. But gardens are different—you cannot make grass and flowers grow just so on short notice! You plant and dig and plant again, before things grow as you have visualized them.

There was a double ring of trees in one corner of our domain, enclosing the *salle de verdure*, or outdoor drawing room. In the center of this enchanted circle there was a statue by Clodion, a joyous nymph, holding a baby faun in her arms. There were several old stone benches under the trees that must have known the secrets of the famous ladies of the eighteenth-century courts. The *salle de verdure* looked just as it did when the little daughters of Louis xv came here to have their afternoon cakes and tea, so we did not try to change this bit of the garden.

My idea of making over the place was to leave the part of the garden against the stone walls in the rear in its tangled, woodsy state, and to build against it a trellis that would be in line with the terrace. Between the trellis and the terrace there was to be a smooth expanse of greensward, bordered with flowers. It seemed very simple, but I hereby confess that I built and tore down the trellis three times before it pleased me! I had to make it worthy of the statue by Pradier that was given to us by Sardou, and finally it was done to please me. Painted a soft green, with ivy growing over it, and a fountain flanked by white marbles outlined against it, this trellis represents (to me, at least) my best work.

The *tapis vert* occupies the greater part of the garden, and it is bordered by gravel walks bordered in turn with white flowerbeds. Between the walks and the walls there are the groups of trees, the statues with green spaces about them, the masses of evergreen trees, and finally the great trees that follow the lines of the wall. Indeed, the *tapis vert* is like the arena of an ample theater, with the ascending flowers and shrubs and trees representing the ascending tiers of seats.

One feels that all the trees and flowers look down upon the central stretch of greensward, and perhaps there is a fairy ring here where plays take place by night. Nothing is impossible in this garden. Certainly the fairies play in the enchanted ring of the trees of the *salle de verdure*. We are convinced of that.

So formal is the *tapis vert*, with its blossoming borders of larkspur and daisies and its tall standard roses, you are surprised to find that that part of the garden outside this prim rectangle has mysteries. There are winding paths that terminate in marble seats. There is the pavillon, a little house built for outdoor musicales, with electric connections that make breakfast and tea possible here. There is the guest house, and the motor house—quite as interesting as any other part of the garden. And everywhere there are blue and white and rose-colored flowers, planted in great masses against the black-green evergreens.

We leave America early in June, tired out with the breathless business of living, and find ourselves in our old-world house and garden. We fall asleep to the accompaniment of the tiny piping of the little people in our garden. We awake to the matins of the birds. We breakfast on the stone terrace, with boughs of trees and clouds for our roof, and as we look out over the masses of blue flowers and the smooth green *tapis vert*, over the arched trelliage with its fountains and its marbles, the great trees back of our domain frame the supremely beautiful towers of the Château le Magnificent, and we are far happier than anyone deserves to be in this wicked world![1]

XX.
NOTES ON MANY THINGS

A LITTLE TALK ON CLOCKS.

THE SELECTION OF PROPER CLOCKS for one's house is always long-drawn-out, a pursuit of real pleasure. Clocks are such necessary things the thoughtless person is apt to compromise, when they don't find exactly the right one. How much wiser and happier they would be if they decided to depend upon an ordinary alarm clock until the proper clock was discovered! If they made a hobby of their quest for clocks they would find much amusement, many other valuable objects by-the-way, and finally exactly the right clocks for their rooms.

Everyone knows the merits and demerits of the hundreds of clocks of commerce, and it isn't for me to go into the subject of grandfather clocks, bracket clocks, and banjo clocks, where there are so many excellent books on the subject. I plead for the graceful clocks of old France, the *objets d'art* so lovingly designed by the master sculptors of the eighteenth century. I plead particularly for the wall clocks that are so conspicuous in all good French houses, and so unusual in our own country.

Just as surely as our fine old English and American have their proper niches, so the French clocks belong inevitably in certain rooms. You may never find just the proper clock for this room, but that is your fault. There are hundreds of lovely old models available. Why shouldn't some manufacturer have them reproduced?

I feel that if people generally knew how very decorative and distinguished a good wall clock may be, the demand would soon create a supply of these beautiful objects. It would be quite simple for the manufacturers to make them from the old models. The late Mr. Pierpont Morgan gave to the Metropolitan Museum the magnificent Hoentschel collection of *objets d'art*, hoping to stimulate the interest of American designers and artisans in the fine models of the seventeenth and eighteenth centuries. There are some very fine examples of wall clocks in this collection, which might be copied in carved wood by the students of manual training schools, if the manufacturers refuse to be interested.

Wall clocks first came into France in the early part of the seventeenth century, and are a part of the furnishings of all the fine old French houses. A number of the most interesting clocks I have picked up were the wooden models, which served for the fine bronze clocks of the eighteenth century. The master designer first worked out his idea in wood before making the clock in bronze, and the wooden models were sold for a song. I have one of these clocks in my dining room. It is as much a part of the wall decoration as the lights or the mirrors.

The wall clocks I like best are fixed directly on the wall, the dial glass opening so that the clock may be wound with a key. I have such a clock in one of my dining rooms. This fine old clock is given the place of honor in the main panel of the wall, above the console table. I often use such a clock in a dining room, just as I use the fine old French mantel clocks in my drawing rooms. These clocks are happily placed, for the marble of the mantel, the lighting fixtures nearby and the fine little bronze busts are all in key with the exquisite workmanship of the clock. In another room in my house, a bedroom, there is a beautiful little French clock that is the only object allowed on the mantel shelf. The beautiful carving of the mirror frame back of it seems a part of the clock, a deliberate background for it.

This is one of the many wall clocks, which were known as bracket clocks, the bracket being as carefully designed and carved as the clock itself. Most of the clocks we see nowadays grew out of the old bracket models.

The American clockmakers of the eighteenth century made many of those jolly little wall clocks called Wag-on-the-Wall. These clocks may still be picked up in out-of-the-way towns. In construction they are very much like the old cuckoo clock which has come to us from Switzerland, and the tile clock which comes from Holland. These clocks with long, exposed weights and pendulum, have not the dignity of the French wall clocks, which were as complete in themselves as fine bas reliefs, and of even greater decorative importance.

Every room in my house has its clock, and to me these magic little instruments have an almost human interest. They seem always friendly to me, whether they mark off the hours that weigh so heavily and seem never-ending, or the happy hours that go all too quickly. I love clocks so much myself that it always astonishes me to go into a room where there is none, or, if there is, it is one of those abortive, exaggerated, gilded clocks that are falsely labeled "French" and sold at a great price in the shops. Somehow, one never expects a clock of this kind to keep time—it is bought as an ornament and if it runs at all it wheezes, or gasps, or makes a dreadful noise, and invariably stops at half-past three.

I am such a crank about good clocks that I take my own with me, even on a railway train. I think I have the smallest clock in the world, which strikes the hours. There are many tiny clocks made which strike if one touches a spring, but my clock always strikes of itself. Cartier, who designed and made this extraordinary timepiece, assures me that he has never seen so small a clock, which strikes. It is very pleasant to have this little clock with its friendly chime with me when I am in some desolate hotel or some strange house.

There are traveling clocks in small leather cases which can be bought very cheaply indeed now, and one of these clocks should be part of everyone's traveling equipment. The humble nickeled watch with a leather case is infinitely better than the pretentious clocks, monstrosities of marble and brass and bad taste.[1]

A CORNER FOR WRITING.

One of my greatest pleasures, when I am planning the furnishing of a house, is the selection and equipment of the necessary writing tables. Every room in every house has its own suggestion for an original treatment, and I enjoy working out a plan for a writing corner that will offer a maximum of convenience, and beauty and charm, for in these busy days we need all these qualities for the inspiration of a pleasant note. You see, I believe in proper writing tables, just as I believe in proper chairs. I have so many desks in my own house that are in constant use, perhaps I can give you my theory best by recording my actual practice of it.

I have spoken of the necessity of a desk in the hallway, and indeed, I have said much of desks in other rooms, but I have still to emphasize my belief in the importance of the equipment of desks.

Of course, one needs a desk in one's own room. Here there is infinite latitude, for there are dozens of delightful possibilities. I always place my desks near the windows. If the wall space is filled, I place an oblong table at right angles to a window, and there you are. In my own private sitting room I have a long desk so placed, in my own house. In a guest room I furnished recently, I used a common oblong table of no value, painted the legs a soft green and covered it with a piece of sage green damask. This is one of the nicest writing tables I know, and it could be copied for a song. The equipment of it is what counts. I used two lamps, dull green jars with mauve silk shades, a dark green leather rack for paper and envelopes, and a great blotter pad that will save the damask from ink spots. The small things are of green pottery and crystal. In a young girl's bedroom I used a sweet little desk of painted wood, a desk that has the naïve charm of innocence. I do hope it inspires the proper love letters.

I always make provision for writing in dressing rooms—a sliding shelf in the dressing table, and a shallow drawer for pencils and paper—and I have adequate writing facilities in the housekeepers' quarters, so that there may be no excuse for forgetting orders or messages. This seems to me absolutely necessary in our modern domestic routine: it is part of the business principle we borrow from the efficient office routine of our corporations. The dining room and the bathrooms are the only places where the writing table, in one form or another, isn't required.

I like the long flat tables or small desks much better than the huge roll-top affairs or the heavy desks built after the fashion of the old armoire. If the room is large enough, a secretary after an eighteenth-century model will be a beautiful and distinguished piece of furniture. I have such a secretary in my own sitting room, a chest of drawers surmounted by a cabinet of shelves with glass doors, but I do not use it as a desk. I use the shelves for my old china and porcelains, and the drawers for pamphlets and the thousand and one things that are too flimsily bound for bookshelves. Of course, if one has a large correspondence and uses one's home as an office, it is better to have a large desk with a top which closes. I prefer tables, and I have them made big enough to hold all my papers, big enough to spread out on.

There are dozens of enchanting small desks that are exactly right for guest rooms, the extremely feminine desks that come from old France. One of the most fascinating ones is copied from a *bureau de toilette* that belonged to Marie Antoinette. In those days the writing of letters and the making of a toilet went together. This old desk has a drawer filled with compartments for toilet things, powders and perfumes and patches, and above this vanity drawer there is the usual shelf for writing, and compartments for paper and letters. The desk itself suggests brocade flounces and powdered hair, so exquisitely is it constructed of tulipwood and inlaid with other woods of many colors.

Then there are the small desks made by modern furniture makers, just large enough to hold a blotting pad, a paper rack, and a pair of candlesticks. There is always a shallow drawer for writing materials. Such a desk may be decorated to match the chintzes of any small bedroom.

If it isn't possible for you to have a desk in each guest room, there should be a little writing room somewhere apart from the family living room. If you live in one of those old-fashioned houses intersected by great halls with much wasted space on the upper floors, you may make a little writing room of one of the hall ends, and screen it from the rest of the hall with a high standing screen. If you have a house of the other extreme type, a city house with little hall bedrooms, use one of these little rooms for a writing room. You will require a desk well-stocked with stationery, and all the things the writer will need; a shelf of address books and reference books—with a dictionary, of course; many pens and pencils and fresh blotters, and so forth. Of course, you may have ever so many more things, but it isn't necessary. Better a quiet corner with one chair and a desk, than the elaborate library with its superb fittings where people come and go.

Given the proper desk, the furnishing of it is most important. The blotting pad should be heavy enough to keep its place, and the blotting paper should be constantly renewed. I know of nothing more offensive than dusty, ink-splotched blotting paper. There are very good sets to be had, now, made of brass, bronze, carved wood, porcelain, silver or crystal, and there are leather boxes for holding stationery and leather portfolios to be had in all colors. I always add to these furnishings a good pair of scissors, stationery marked with the house address or the monogram of the person to whom the desk especially belongs, an almanac, and a pincushion! My pincushions are as much a part of the equipment of a desk as the writing things, and they aren't frilly, ugly things. They are covered with brocade or damask or some stuff used elsewhere in the room and I assure you they are most useful. I find that pins are almost as necessary as pens in my correspondence; they are much more expedient than pigeon-holes.

In country houses I think it shows forethought and adds greatly to the comfort of the guests to have a small framed card showing the arrival and departure of trains and of mails, especially if the house is a great distance from the railway station. This saves much inquiry and time. In the paper rack there should be not only stamped paper bearing the address of the house, telephone number, and so forth, but also telegraph blanks, post cards, stamps, and so forth. Very often people who have beautiful places have post cards made showing various views of the house and garden.

Test the efficiency of your writing tables occasionally by using them yourself. This is the only way to be sure of the success of anything in your house—try it yourself.

STOOLS AND BENCHES.

I often wonder, when I grope my way through drawing rooms crowded and jammed with chairs and sofas, why more people do not realize the advantages of stools and benches. A well-made stool is doubly useful: it may be used to sit upon or it may be used to hold a tray, or whatever you please. It is really preferable to a small table because it is not aways full of a nondescript collection of ornaments, which seems to be the fate of all small tables. It has also the advantage of being low enough to push under a large table, when need be, and it occupies much less space than a chair apparently (not actually) because it has no back. I have stools, or benches, or both in all my rooms, because I find them convenient and easily moved about, but I have noticed an amusing thing: Whenever a fat person comes to see me, he or she always sits on the smallest stool in the room. I have many fat friends, and many stools, but invariably the fattest person gravitates to the smallest stool.

The stools I like best for the drawing room are the fine old ones, covered with needlework or brocade, but there are many simpler ones of plain wood with cane insets that are very good for other rooms. Then there are the long banquettes, or benches, which are so nice in drawing rooms and hallways and nicest of all in a ballroom. Indeed, a ballroom needs no other movable furniture, given plenty of these long benches. They may be of the very simplest description, but when used in a fine room should be covered with a good damask or velvet or some rich fabric.

I have a fine eighteenth-century banquette in my drawing room, the frame being carved and gilded and the seat covered with Venetian red velvet. You will find these gilded stools all over England. There are a number at Hampton Court Palace. At Hardwick there are both long and short stools, carved with the dolphin's scroll and covered with elaborate stuffs.

The older the English house, the more stools are in evidence. In the early sixteenth century joint stools were used in every room. In the bedrooms they served the purposes of small tables and chairs as well. There are ever so many fine old walnut stools and the lower stools used for bed-steps to be bought in London shops that make a specialty of old English furniture, and reproductions of them may be bought in the better American shops. I often wonder why we do not see more bedside stools. They are so convenient, even though the bed be only moderately high from the floor. Many of mine are only six inches high, about the height of a fat floor cushion.

Which reminds me: the floor cushion, made of the same velvet made for carpeting, is a modern luxury we can't afford to ignore. Lately I have seen such beautiful ones, about three feet long and one foot wide, covered in tapestry, with great gold tassels at the corners. The possibilities of the floor cushion idea are limitless. They take the place of the usual footstool in front of the boudoir easy chair, or beside the day bed or *chaise-longue*, or beside the large bed, for that matter. They are no longer unsanitary, because with vacuum cleaners they may be kept as clean as chair cushions. They may be made to fit into almost any room. I saw a half-dozen of them in a dining room, recently, small square hard ones, covered with the gold-colored velvet of the carpet. They were not more than four or five inches thick, but that is the ideal height for an under-the-table cushion. Try it.

PORCELAIN STOVES.

When the Colony Club was at last finished we discovered that the furnace heat did not go up to the roof garden, and immediately we had to find some way of heating this very attractive and very necessary space. Even from the beginning we were sadly crowded for room, so popular was the clubhouse, and the roof garden was much needed for the overflow. We conferred with architects, builders and plumbers, and found it would be necessary to spend about seven thousand dollars and to close the club for about two months in order to carry the heating arrangements up to the roof. This was disastrous for a new club, already heavily in arrears and running under heavy expenses. I worried and worried over the situation, and suddenly one night an idea came to me: I remembered some great porcelain stoves I had seen in Germany. I felt that these stoves were exactly what we needed, and that we should be rescued from an embarrassing situation without much trouble or expense. I was just leaving for Europe, so I hurried on to the manufacturers of these wonderful stoves and found, after much difficulty, a model that seemed practicable, and not too huge in proportion. The model, unfortunately, was white with gilded garlands, far too French and magnificent for our sun room. I persuaded them to make two of the stoves for me in green Majolica, with garlands of soft-toned flowers, and finally we achieved just the stoves for the room.

But my troubles were not over: when the stoves reached New York, we tried to take them up to the roof, and found them too large for the stairs. We couldn't have them lifted up by pulleys, because the glass walls of the roof garden and the fretwork at the top of the roof made it impossible for the workers to get "purchase" for their pulleys. Finally we persuaded a gentleman who lived next door to let us take them over the roof of his house, and the deed was accomplished. The stoves were equal to the occasion. They heated the roof garden perfectly, and were of great decorative value.

Encouraged by this success I purchased another porcelain stove, this time a cream-colored porcelain one, and used it in a hallway in an uptown house. It was the one thing needed to give the hall great distinction. Since then I have used a number of these stoves, and I wonder why our American manufacturers do not make them. They are admirable for heating difficult rooms—outdoor porches, and draughty halls, and rooms not heated by furnaces. The stoves are becoming harder and harder to find, though I was fortunate enough to purchase one last year from the Marchioness of Anglesey, who was giving up her home at Versailles. This stove was of white Majolica with little Loves in terra cotta adorning it. The new ones are less attractive, but it would be perfectly simple to have any tile manufacturer copy an old one, given the design.

Wall fountains as we know them are introduced into our modern houses for their decorative interest and for the joy they give us, the joyous sound and color of falling water. We use them because they are beautiful and cheerful, but originally they had a most definite purpose. They were built into the walls of the dining halls in medieval times, and used for washing the precious plate.

If you look into the history of any *objet d'art* you will find that it was first used for a purpose. All the superb masterly things that have come to us had logical beginnings. It has remained for the thoughtless designer of our times to produce things of no use and no meaning. The old designers decorated the small objects of daily use as faithfully as they decorated the greater things, the wall spaces and ceilings and great pieces of furniture, and so this little wall basin which began in such a homely way soon became a beautiful thing.

Europe has countless small fountains built for interior walls and for small alcoves and indoor conservatories, but we are just beginning to use them in America. American sculptors are doing such notable work, however, that we shall soon plan our indoor fountains as carefully as we plan our fireplaces. The fact that our houses are heated mechanically has not lessened our appreciation of an open fire, and running water brought indoors has the same animate charm.

I have a wall fountain in the entrance hall of my own New York house in East Fifty-fifth Street. I have had this wall fountain built as part of the architectural detail of the room, with a background of paneled mirrors. It spills over into a marble-curbed pool where fat, orange-colored goldfish live. I keep the fountain banked with flowers. You can imagine the pleasure of leaving the dusty city streets and entering this cool, pleasant entrance hall.

Our modern use of indoor fountains is perfectly legitimate: we use them to bring the atmosphere of outdoors in. In country houses we use fountains in our gardens, but in the city we have no gardens, and so we are very wise to bring in the outdoor things that make our lives a little more gay and informal. The more suggestive of out-of-doors the happier is the effect of the sun room. Occasionally, one sees a rare house where a glass-enclosed garden opens from one of the living rooms. There is a house in Nineteenth Street that has such an enclosed garden, built around a wall fountain. The garden opens out of the great two-storied music room. Lofty windows flank a great door, and fill the end of the room with a luminous composition of leaded glass. Through the door you enter the garden, with its tiled floor, its glass ceiling, and its low brick retaining walls. The wall fountain is placed exactly in front of the great door, and beneath it there is a little semi-circular pool bordered with plants and glittering with goldfish. Evergreens are banked against the brick walls, and flat reliefs are hung just under the glass ceiling. The garden is quite small, but takes its place as an important part of the room. It rivals in interest the massive Gothic fireplace, with its huge logs and feudal fire irons.

The better silversmiths are doing much to encourage the development of indoor fountains. They display the delightful fountains of our young American sculptors, fountains that would make any garden room notable. There are so many of these small bronze fountains, with Pan piping his irresistible tune of outdoors; children playing with frogs or geese or lizards or turtles; gay little figures prancing in enchanted rings of friendly beasties. Why don't we make use of them?

THE END

ILLUSTRATIONS

The private dining room in the Colony Club

A Colony Club bedroom

The staircase in the Bayard Thayer House

A fine old console in the Villa Trianon

A wallpaper of Elizabethan design with oak furniture

Built-in bookshelves in a small room

Miss Crocker's Louis XVI bed

Fine old French wall light for candles

Miss Anne Morgan's Louis XVI dressing room

Miss Morgan's Louis XVI lit de repos

Miss Morgan's Louis XVI boudoir

A Washington Irving House bedroom

Muslin glass curtains in the Washington Irving House

A Chinese Chippendale sofa covered with chintz

A painted wall broken into panels by narrow moldings

Portrait by Nattier inset above a fine old mantel

In this hall, simplicity, suitability and proportion are observed

NOTES

CHAPTER I.

1. Later in the twentieth century, the idea of a "female" interior and a husband or boyfriend living as a perpetual "houseguest" gave way to exactly what de Wolfe had strove for since the turn of the century: equality of the sexes. Nowhere is this equality more evident today than as reflected by our interiors.

2. Computer-aided design (CAD) software has drained much of the individuality out of our architecture. Today, architects or designers select moldings, window or door styles, railings or balustrades from computer menus, and the options are all equally disproportionate and out of character of the house being designed.

3. De Wolfe worked tirelessly for women's suffrage when this book was first published, and in the decorative élan singlehandedly created careers in which women could excel. Little did she know that by the end of the century, she would spawn a legion of men who followed in her footsteps and precepts. Knowing this, she would no doubt have recognized the "intimate and charming" interiors created by the seventeenth-century chevalier Bussy de Rabutin, or the delightfully scaled eighteenth-century interiors at the Desert de Retz created by Monsieur de Monville. She also would have considered the charming nineteenth-century interiors of the Count Potocki or those of her friends (to whom she was both mentor and mother superior) and the twentieth-century arbiters, Tony Duquette, Cecil Beaton, Carlos de Beistegui, and Billy Baldwin.

4. These superb apartments were more than likely planned jointly by Isabella d'Este and Michaelangelo, whom she often employed to design her *fêtes*, as well as embroidery of her undergarments.

5. Interest in late nineteenth-century decorative arts has grown since *The House in Good Taste*'s first publication. De Wolfe's "hated" Eastlake walnut and cocobolo and the pickle-and-plum-colored Morris furniture are not only highly collectible but prized by museums and designers around the world, the subject of numerous books. De Wolfe simply didn't like Victorian—the high style of her sad childhood—and chose to banish it from her design vocabulary.

6. De Wolfe's taste constantly grew and evolved, and the by the 1920s she embraced Art Deco, her permanent apartment on Avenue D'lena in Paris being a fine example. By 1942 she championed the burgeoning neo-baroque style exemplified by rococo plasterwork and *trompe l'oeil* effects.

CHAPTER II.

1. When *The House in Good Taste* was first published, electric lighting was somewhat of a novelty in many interiors. De Wolfe would have embraced all of the latest advances in lighting technology, from ceiling spots to halogen. She believed in indirect lighting and thick paper shades that did not permit light to pass sideways. She was also very fond of candlelight. In the early 1940s, de Wolfe discovered and sponsored Mr. Wendel's "Wendel Lighting," which has become the hallmark of the perfectly lighted room today.

2. Were de Wolfe alive today, she would invariably have included a paragraph about "air conditioning" and its health hazards. She would also applaud and endorse the advances in forced-air heat, radiant heat, and climate-controlled rooms through computer technology.

3. At the time of publication, "paper floors and iron ceilings" were the equivalent of today's tawdry wall-to-wall nylon shag carpeting and sprayed-on cottage-cheese ceilings.

4. Later in the twentieth century, the gaudy opulence of "Marie Antoinette rooms" was re-christened "Le Style Rothschild."

5. After this book was published a new style was born, Art Deco, which Elsie de Wolfe embraced with enthusiasm.

6. In 1941 de Wolfe succumbed to a neo-baroque decorative style for her Beverly Hills house, After All, incorporating "chairs whose legs were fashioned like aquatic plants, tables upheld by tortured naked women or blackamoores as the case may be, lighting fixtures in the form of tassels and other theatrical decorative effects."

CHAPTER III.

1. De Wolfe, like so many interior designers after her, "listened" to her house. The Washington Irving House "spoke to her, and she heard it."

2. De Wolfe did not merely go in and all at once do the Irving House's entrance hall, but rather solved the décor problems as she encountered them. She considered the house a living thing, and she needed to "deceive the old hall into thinking itself a spacious thing," and she innately realized the importance of all five senses to her interiors. By upholstering the stair rail with velvet, she introduced the sense of touch as well as sight to the entrance hall.

3. De Wolfe's early insistence on working with an architect to ensure that all the bones of the house were in the right place in order to support her ideas for the décor began with this project.

4. It is often interesting to trace the loves of a designer or collector through his or her use of possessions in multiple houses over a period of years. In her personal homes, de Wolfe repeatedly used the same sofa again, a prized pair of silver candlesticks, various oil paintings, and favorite materials or treasured objects.

5. The "French things" de Wolfe defends here were also lightweight and easy to move to create groupings for conversation, a marked contrast to the preferred heavy and dark-stained Victorian furniture popular at the time. Her French things had delicately carved frames and light painted finishes, which, although old, gave a new look to the American interior.

6. Creating interiors by incorporating "new inventions" such as electric light and telephones and learning where to place them for convenience and function set de Wolfe apart from her contemporaries. Before she found suitable placement of these modern conveniences, they were placed at the whim of a workman without thought to how they would be used and, for the most part, they were placed sparingly. One electrical outlet per room was considered to be enough.

7. When de Wolfe decorated this bedroom for Elizabeth Marbury, chintz was considered a material suitable only for the housekeeper's rooms in America. De Wolfe introduced the idea of using these inexpensive and often beautifully printed cottons for a house's principle rooms, adopted after visiting her aristocratic English friends. Today, chintz manufacturers must light a candle nightly to de Wolfe, for her inexpensive chintz has become an expensive decorating status symbol.

CHAPTER IV.

1. This house, which still exists much as de Wolfe remodeled it, is located at 123 East Fifty-Fifth Street in New York City. To achieve this remarkable transformation, de Wolfe called upon talented young architect Ogden Codman, who had previously written with Edith Wharton *The Decoration of Houses* in an attempt to alter the heavy Victorian tastes of the day.

2. Today's mega-mansions often require assistance to maintain them. Although these houses contain modest housekeepers' quarters, it is rare to find space for a complete live-in staff as in de Wolfe's day. What is important to note, however, is de Wolfe's attention to the placement of the housekeepers' rooms their correlation to and connections with other areas of the house: kitchen, laundry, storerooms and pantry. I cannot tell you how many times I have reviewed proposed building plans for houses, only to ask the architect and the owners how they intended to get their groceries from the garage to the kitchen without going through the entire house, or how they intended to serve dinner in the dining room when the kitchen was across a hall two rooms away! For those of us living without household help, the importance of proper room placement is equally important, and possibly more so. We have to move easily between rooms while seeing to ourselves and our guests. The butler's pantry (with or without a butler) and the separation of the kitchen from the dining room are the most important—and most often forgotten—considerations in modern homes.

CHAPTER V.

1. The problem of the picture rail has evaded the modern house. For the most part, we hang our pictures directly on the walls, although several modern systems exist whereby people may hang paintings from the ceiling or crown moldings without using hammers and nails.

CHAPTER VI.

1. De Wolfe consistently compared color to music, even though she famously couldn't carry a tune and preferred to play cards rather than endure a drawing-room music performance. Nevertheless, she backed the first musicals of her friends Cole Porter and Jerome Kern, participating in the birth of the Broadway musical. Her favorite song was "People Will Say We're in Love" from *Oklahoma!*, which she would "murder" for friends. Her color sense was, naturally, superb—although she was the champion of the all-white room, the black-and-white room, and announced upon seeing the Parthenon, "Beige, my color!"

CHAPTER X.

1. De Wolfe never had a piano in her homes, not even the Villa Trianon or After All. She would hire a piano if the evening called for it, but she never capitulated on regarding the piano a disaster of decoration. She felt little more for the dining room—"the most useless room in the house," she would say. De Wolfe preferred to dine all over the house and in the garden. She opposed rooms that served but one purpose—to which her cocktail parties served in the bathroom indubitably attest.

CHAPTER XI.

1. De Wolfe loved open fires, and installed fireplaces in every possible room in her houses, including the bathrooms at the Villa Trianon and her Paris apartment.

CHAPTER XII.

1. The home office has become an essential room in the modern interior, and whether it is a man's or woman's domain, it needs to be a functional and well laid-out area for conducting business.

CHAPTER XV.

1. De Wolfe put most of these ideas into use at her Villa Trianon, her design laboratory. When she was restoring the old house, she informed the contractor that she wanted a separate bathroom for each bedroom. The contractor told her that not only was it impossible, but probably illegal! De Wolfe won, and each of the five bedrooms has a proper bath, but for whatever reasons the clothes closets remained in the attic. Moreover, these wardrobes lacked closet poles. All the closets at Villa Trianon held only hooks placed along the walls—no poles, no shelves. She also installed a swimming pool that doubled as a reflecting pool and fountain at the villa, as well as a trellised pool pavilion with changing rooms. This pavilion doubled as a space where she entertained with concerts and a cinema.

CHAPTER XVI.

1. De Wolfe spoke from experience regarding apartment living. At the penthouse apartment she built for herself on the Avenue d'Iena in Paris, she created a compact and modern space for efficient living. Later, in America, she stayed in a series of New York hotel suites, which she designed as a backdrop for herself and her ideas for living with the bare essentials, even though such "bare essentials" were supplied by Prince Serge Obolensky and the St. Regis Hotel.

CHAPTER XVII.

1. One of de Wolfe's most important contributions to modern American decorating was the way she embraced quality reproduction furniture. Although her own houses were furnished almost exclusively with genuine antiques, she recognized the value of good decorative pieces and their suitability for people wishing to furnish houses within a budget. Interestingly, her hatred of Victorian furniture in 1913 turned around by the 1940s, when she created a vogue for Victorian furnishings (usually painted white) as amusing accents for her newly theatrical neo-baroque green and white interiors.

CHAPTER XVIII.

1. De Wolfe often said that the trelliage screen in the garden at the Villa Trianon was her finest work. Later she added mirrors to her trellised fantasies to extend the vistas in her gardens. Her unconventional use of mirrors on her houses' exteriors became one of her many decorative trademarks.

CHAPTER XIX.

1. De Wolfe never stopped working on the Villa Trianon and its gardens; she returned there after World War II, and continued improving the property until her death in 1950. The tangled garden near the stone wall was the sight of her dog cemetery, each tombstone reading, "the one I loved the best." The stone terrace was later "glassed in" to provide an elegantly furnished and mirrored winter garden. With Ann Morgan, a wing was added, consisting of a long ballroom with a formal bedroom, which she called "le chambre de parade." In 1940 de Wolfe added another ballroom, this one in the shape of a circus tent built of concrete and glass but painted to resemble green-and-white striped canvas. Complete with a dance floor and working fireplace, it was one of de Wolfe's last major additions to the property.

CHAPTER XX.

1. One of de Wolfe's greatest treasures was a little gold clock in red enamel—a gift from Henry Clay Frick upon the completion of his family apartments in what is now New York's Frick Collection.

ACKNOWLEDGMENTS

This publication would not be possible without the gracious collaboration of the Elsie de Wolfe Foundation, Arnold Palmer, Patsy Palmer, Ruth Wilkinson, Hutton Wilkinson, Charles Silverberg, Sally Schneider, Albert Hadley, Joseph Holtzman, Stan Abercrombie, Linda O'Keeffe, John Esten, W.B. McCabe and Beth Daugherty at Potterton Books.

A special thanks to: Charles Miers, Eva Prinz, Jacqueline Byrnes, Ellen Nidy and Pam Sommers at Rizzoli International Publications, and to David Elson and Andrew Prinz at the Simultaneous Workshop, who designed this book.

Illustrations reprinted from the original edition of *The House In Good Taste* from the archives of the Elsie de Wolfe Foundation, photographer unknown. Courtesy of the Elsie de Wolfe Foundation.

ABOUT THE AUTHOR

Elsie de Wolfe (1865-1950) was born in New York City. She was an actress, decorator, and hostess. The career in which she achieved distinction was one she created for herself and other women. At the suggestion of her closest friend, Elizabeth Marbury, she turned her interest in interior design into a profession, becoming America's first female decorator. With the original publication of *The House in Good Taste* she became an arbiter of American design.

ABOUT HUTTON WILKINSON

Hutton Wilkinson was born in Los Angeles, California and grew up in the architectural offices of his father and grandfather. At eighteen he had the opportunity to apprentice under the great American design icon, Tony Duquette. In 1997, Wilkinson and Duquette started a fine jewelry company. As owner and design director of this enterprise, Wilkinson continues to market these unique jeweled creations internationally. Wilkinson is the president of the Elsie de Wolfe Foundation.

ABOUT ALBERT HADLEY

Albert Hadley was born in Nashville, Tennessee. After World War II he moved to New York to attend and graduate from The Parsons School of Design. In 1962, he began his legendary association with Mrs. Henry "Sister" Parish II. In 1999, Albert Hadley closed the doors of Parish-Hadley and once again began his own firm, Albert Hadley, Incorporated.